David Van Horne

Tent and saddle life in the Holy Land

David Van Horne

Tent and saddle life in the Holy Land

ISBN/EAN: 9783337283605

Printed in Europe, USA, Canada, Australia, Japan

Cover: Foto ©Lupo / pixelio.de

More available books at www.hansebooks.com

TENT AND SADDLE LIFE

IN THE

HOLY LAND.

BY

REV. DAVID VAN HORNE, D.D.,

AUTHOR OF
"THE MOUNTAIN BOY OF WILDHAUS; A LIFE OF ULRIC ZWINGLI," ETC.

PHILADELPHIA:
THE AMERICAN SUNDAY-SCHOOL UNION,
1122 CHESTNUT STREET.
1885.

PREFACE.

Our chief interest in the Holy Land arises from its association with the Bible. The country once trodden by the patriarchs, judges, kings and prophets, and by the Saviour himself and the apostles, cannot fail to attract the attention of travellers and readers in each generation. Besides this the face of the country is diversified, and the scenery of more than passing interest.

After our passage tickets had been purchased a rumor of the outbreak of the plague, on the shores of the Black Sea, threatened to interfere with our journey. The consequent falling off in the number of travellers eventually proved an advantage to our small party of three clergymen, since we enjoyed quite a monopoly of the arrangements made for a larger number, giving us a choice of guides, provisions and horses. We were also more free to make little excursions aside from the main lines of travel, and could obtain full replies to our questions from the dragomans. A kind Providence preserved us from the rumored pestilence.

The results of our observations there are laid

before the reader in the following pages. Many travellers have gone over these pathways of the Holy Land, and have given valuable descriptions of the country and its inhabitants. Each observer gains new views, his descriptions shed fresh light upon the teachings of Scripture, and thus, as by work on a grand mosaic, the picture of the land is to be gradually completed.

The incidents of tent and saddle life narrated here may serve to interest youthful readers, and are inserted in the hope of securing their attention. The experiences in camp, and the novelty of the sights by the wayside, the strange dress and manners of the people, and the old-fashioned methods of labor and travel, kept us constantly on the alert, and we trust that some of this interest will be shared by the reader.

The critical notes furnished by Rev. Edwin W. Rice, D.D., Editor of the American Sunday-School Union, add largely to the value of the book for the advanced reader. In them will be found the results of the latest researches of the "Western Palestine Survey," "Conder's Tent Work" and other fresh authorities. The excellent illustrations furnished by the publishers (many of them, by permission, from Schaff's Dictionary of the Bible) will lend additional interest to the work.

CONTENTS.

CHAPTER I.
Landing at Jaffa, ... 9

CHAPTER II.
Sharon and Ramleh, ... 22

CHAPTER III.
Going up to Jerusalem, ... 37

CHAPTER IV.
Sights on Mount Moriah, ... 54

CHAPTER V.
Tour to Hebron, ... 78

CHAPTER VI.
From Hebron to Bethlehem, ... 104

CHAPTER VII.
Walks about Zion, ... 116

CHAPTER VIII.
Olivet and Bethany, ... 130

CHAPTER IX.
Tour to Mizpeh and Gibeon, ... 143

CHAPTER X.
Tour to the Dead Sea and the Jordan, . . 161

CHAPTER XI.
From Jericho to the Valley of Baca, . . . 183

CHAPTER XII.
From Baca to the Vale of Nablus, . . . 201

CHAPTER XIII.
From Nablus to Jenin, ... 221

CHAPTER XIV.
Around the Great Plain of Esdraelon, . . 236

CHAPTER XV.
Nazareth, ... 255

CHAPTER XVI.
Tabor and Tiberias, ... 271

CHAPTER XVII.
Around the Lake of Galilee—The Plain of Gennesaret, ... 285

CHAPTER XVIII.
Around the Lake of Galilee—Bethsaida and Capernaum, ... 302

CHAPTER XIX.
The Valley of the Huleh, ... 319

CHAPTER XX.
Dan and Banias, ... 332

LIST OF ILLUSTRATIONS.

American Consulate at Jerusalem,	Frontispiece.
Yafa (Joppa) from the Sea,	11
Exterior of the supposed House of Simon the Tanner,	14
Traditional Tomb of Dorcas at Jaffa,	25
Tower at Er-Ramleh,	32
Inn or Khan,	37
Kuryet el Enab (Kirjath-jearim),	44
The Interior of the Jaffa Gate,	53
Modern Jerusalem,	55
The Mosque of Omar and the Haram Area,	60
Eastern Wall of Jerusalem and Muslim Tombs,	67
Traditional Pool of Bethesda,	70
Ecce Homo Arch, Via Dolorosa,	75
The Wailing-place of the Jews,	77
Tomb of Rachel, near Bethlehem,	82
Eastern Mourners at the Grave,	83
Solomon's Pools,	87
Eastern Sheepfold,	90
Eastern Plough,	93
View of Hebron from the South,	97
Mosque at Hebron, covering the Cave at Machpelah,	99
Vineyard in Syria,	105
Bethlehem,	109
View of Jerusalem from the South,	117
Tomb of David,	121
Pool of Hezekiah, inside the Jaffa Gate,	122
Interior of the Church of the Holy Sepulchre,	125
Pool of Siloam,	131
Absalom's Tomb,	132
Mount of Olives,	134
Bethany,	137
Tomb of the Judges,	144

LIST OF ILLUSTRATIONS.

El Jib (Gibeon),	150
Rolling Stone before Tomb,	157
Needle's Eye,	160
The Salt or Dead Sea,	169
Pilgrim's Bathing-place—The River Jordan,	173
Reeds,	175
Inhabitants and Dwellings at Eriha,	179
'Ain es Sultan, or Fountain of Elisha,	183
The Dead Sea from Jebel Usdum, south end,	188
Sycamore,	190
Mountains of Moab,	195
Seilun (ancient Shiloh),	204
Jacob's Well,	211
Nablûs (Shechem),	220
Ruins of the Colonnade of Samaria,	228
Zer'in (site of ancient Jezreel),	237
Date-palm,	239
Nazareth,	254
Place of Elijah's Sacrifice,	260
Lily,	265
Scarlet Lily,	265
Mount Tabor,	270
The Sea of Galilee from Tiberias,	281
Sketch Map of the Sea of Galilee,	286
Gennesaret from Khan Minieh,	299
Tent Life,	301
Mill at Tabighah,	305
Fish of Galilee,	308
Ruins at Tell Hum,	310
Lake Hulch, or Waters of Merom, from the Southwest,	324
Yoke in Use in Palestine,	325
Women Grinding at the Mill in the East,	335
Sources of the Jordan, near Banias,	341
Banias, or Cæsarea-Philippi,	345

TENT AND SADDLE LIFE

IN THE

HOLY LAND.

CHAPTER I.

LANDING AT JAFFA.

A LONG stretch of sandy coast overhung by a steel-gray sky, with glintings of the sunrise behind it; a town perched upon a rocky promontory, with houses reaching down to the water's edge,—this is what we beheld from the deck of the steamer off the port of Yâfa or Jaffa. It was the morning of the last day of March, and, as is usual at that season, scuds of wind and rain were sweeping up and over the coast of Philistia. The sea was rough, and the prospect of getting safe to shore anything but assuring. Here was the entry port to the Holy Land, the very "gate" of the "gorgeous East," which, night and day, by sea and land, we had been seeking, and all the spice of adventure, the view of ancient sites and holy places, the life of tent and saddle, which had been long in anticipation, lay beyond this gateway to Palestine.

And so the half mile of surf between us and the land must be crossed, however hazardous the experiment. It was somewhere here that the prophet Jonah was in deadly peril, and we had often read that this port was unsafe for landing passengers; but, despite all this, we must make the venture. The crew of our vessel had scarcely cast the anchor ere we beheld a number of clumsy boats, with four oars and a helm to each, putting out from the shore. By this time the sea was running high, and as the rollers swept over the jagged reef which fringes the coast, there was danger that the boats would be upset or dashed in pieces. One by one, however, they passed through the narrow opening in the reef, and, in a staggering way, came on to our vessel. After many of the boats filled with the pilgrim passengers from amidship had departed, ten cabin passengers, ourselves among the number, were handed rather unceremoniously into the craft awaiting us.

We were soon tossed up and down like an egg-shell on the angry surf, which frequently dashed into the boat, and withal a heavy shower came on, and wet us through and through. At last we were driven through the narrow passage between

Yafa (Joppa) from the Sea. (*After a photograph.*)

the reefs, and by the mercy of a favoring providence reached the land in safety. Upon leaving the wharf, we were huddled together in a dark cellar, named by courtesy a custom-house, and, dripping wet as we were, waited until our luggage was examined with a "silver key." Through the one narrow, slippery street we next went to the "Mediterranean Hotel," far distant in the German suburb.

According to Josephus, Jaffa originally belonged to the Phœnicians. It has had a secular as well as a sacred history, and from remote times has been the sea-port of southern Palestine. Its name originally meant "delightful" or "beautiful," in the same sense conveyed by the Hebrew word used by Solomon in the "Canticles."* From this came the name "Japho," used in the days when Hiram landed here his rafts of cedar for Solomon's temple at Jerusalem.† Still later, in the time of Jonah, it was known as Joppa, as it was also in the days of the apostle Peter.

As may be imagined, the sad plight we were in did not favor sight-seeing during this our first walk in Palestine. We hastened to the shelter awaiting us, thankful for the comfort of a fire and a change of garments. Luncheon was soon prepared and despatched, and, the storm

---

* Solomon's Song 6 : 4. † 2 Chronicles 2 : 16.

having now passed away, we sallied forth to examine the few points of interest in Jaffa. We found the streets still wet and slippery from the recent shower, and as they were paved for only part of the distance, and in that part only with cobble or field stones, we found the walking anything but pleasant.

EXTERIOR OF THE SUPPOSED HOUSE OF SIMON THE TANNER. (From *Schaff's Dictionary of the Bible*, by permission.)

The open space is the little courtyard at the rear of the house, between the house and the wall overlooking the sea. The spectator has his back to the sea. The well from which Peter is said to have baptized is sunk in the ground on the right.

Under the conduct of our guide, we first visited the traditional site of the house of Simon the tanner, mentioned in the Acts of the Apostles.* The house, in part at least, is a modern structure, built, like the surrounding dwellings, of stone, with a flat roof, having a little low dome in the centre. Upon entering it, we found a large stone trough in the lower story, at one end of which

* Acts 9 : 43 ; 10 : 6.

was a well, with an old axle having four arms by which it was turned in drawing water. This well, it is alleged, was anciently used by Simon in his trade, but now seems to be used only for the ordinary purposes of a household. The property is in the possession of the Mohammedans, who have set apart one room as a place of prayer. This room was small and poorly lighted, dingy and altogether uninviting.

From this point we ascended to the roof by an ancient flight of stone steps, which may indeed, with the foundations of the building, have come down from the times of the apostles. From the roof we enjoyed a very fine view of the surrounding buildings, and the yet turbulent sea breaking upon the ragged edges of the reef, where we had so lately made our dangerous passage.

We were reminded of the classical story of Andromeda, who has a constellation of stars named after her, who, according to the myth, was chained to these very rocks upon which we were gazing. The story runs that Neptune, being enraged because the mother of Andromeda had boasted that she was herself more beautiful than any of his nymphs, sent a frightful sea monster to ravage the country. The oracle of Jupiter Ammon had declared that the only way to appease the anger of Neptune was to expose Andromeda to the devouring monster, which was accordingly done. At the critical moment Perseus appeared, and of course set the maiden free, and afterward married her. The lively imagination of the Greeks still impresses itself upon the world's attention, for we read this story in the constellations which adorn the northern heavens each clear November evening. Whether the old sea monster were still raging around Jaffa on the day of our visit or not, true it was that, like the fair Andromeda, we were in peril among these rocks, although we were not in chains as she is reputed to have been.

From the recollection of this ancient legend, or "fable" as Josephus calls it,* our minds reverted to the glorious fact recorded in Scripture that Peter was praying here, near this very spot, when he had the vision in which he saw the heaven opened and a vessel descending upon the earth, wherein were all manner of four-footed beasts and creeping things and fowls of heaven. In this "vision of toleration," as it has well been named, Peter was instructed to hold fellowship with Gentile converts to Christianity in the words, "What God hath cleansed, *that* call not thou common."† Here at Jaffa, where the Jewish

---

* Wars of Jews 3 : 9, ₰ 3.   † Acts 10 : 11–15.

nation came in contact with the outside world, it was fitting that this remarkable revelation should be made. The vast consequences which have flowed from that single event, and the bearing it has had upon us who are of Gentile extraction, must secure for Jaffa and the house of Simon the tanner a lasting place in the world's history.

The roof of this building afforded us a commanding view of the whole coast-line north and south. A court or yard is attached to the house, with a low wall at its farther side, against which the waves dash in rough weather; and within the court is the well used, as is said, for a long time for the purposes of the tanner. We could see no good reason for doubting the tradition which locates Peter's vision at or near this place, though its identity has often been questioned.

On our way back to the hotel we passed a fine building, beautifully situated upon the high promontory, where the school of Miss Arnold, an English lady, maintains its well-earned reputation. Besides this institution Jaffa boasts of three convents, each of which represents one of the three Christian sects most numerous in Palestine—the Greek, the Latin and the Armenian; and in addition it has two or three Mohammedan mosques. The whole population probably does not exceed five thousand.

Near the city gate we found the bazaar, or market-place for the sale of breadstuffs and the fruits for which the place has ever been famous; and just beyond the city gate, where the road to the northeast diverges from the road to Ramleh, we found the horse-market. Here are the stables of the muleteers, where tourists, unless otherwise provided for, must pass the ordeal of obtaining escorts and animals to convey them to Jerusalem. The mixed multitude were bargaining in horses, camels and donkeys.

All traces of the late shower had now passed away, and the native dragomans, with gay tarbooshes on their heads, flaming sashes about their waists, booted and spurred like knights of errantry, were hurrying hither and thither in preparation for the departure of the caravans. At another point a lady tourist was mounted on a sorry-looking steed, testing the qualities of the animal, while the eloquent guide assured her of his entire trustworthiness, a fact which even the casual observer would not dispute. The scene was altogether novel; the peculiar costumes, mixed language and dashing horsemanship of the natives affording us an anticipation of rich experiences in this line yet in store for us.

Jaffa does not differ from other sea-ports in having people within its walls of different nationalities, and unfortunately this leads to lawlessness and more or less disorder in society, which the Turkish authorities as usual are unable to control or suppress. Accordingly there is but slight security here for life and property, and but little inducement for strangers to take up their permanent abode either in the town or the fine country districts surrounding it.

The attempts at colonization here and at Jerusalem, made at different times since the days of the Crusades, have signally failed. In 1866 forty families came to Jaffa from the state of Maine, and formed what was known as the American colony. Their motive appears to have been partly religious and partly secular. They thought it the duty of Christians in other countries to occupy the Holy Land—not by conquest, as was the thought of the Crusaders, but by purchase—and by careful tillage to restore the soil to its ancient fertility.

The chief drawback to this venture was not in any natural defect of the climate or soil, for both are most favorable to the purposes of immigration. The plain of Sharon evidently is an excellent soil for wheat, millet and other crops, and here as fine orange orchards are found as one can see in the state of Florida or elsewhere. But the sole obstacle to immigration and prosperity here is the lack of good government. No farmer can live in a land where he has no protection for his family, his crops or his cattle.

After a few years the American colony fell into great poverty, and its members would gladly have returned had they had the means. At last a wealthy traveller, who saw their pitiable condition, paid the passage homeward of many sick women and children, and sent them back to America. A few, however, remained, and their sons, who can speak both Arabic and English, are now serving as guides to travellers.

A German colony also came here in 1868 from Wurtemberg, which formed a sect known as the "German Temple." Their distinctive doctrine, founded on some of the prophecies, is that Christians are under an obligation to settle in Palestine. They number about two hundred and fifty souls, part of whom live at Sarona, two miles northeastward and not far from Sir M. Montefiore's garden.

There is another German colony at Jerusalem, founded by Rev. Christopher Hoffman, that came there some years since with the thought of preparing for the second coming of Christ, which they believed to be near at hand. There is also a colony of four hundred Germans near Haifa, under the shadow of Mount Carmel. They are said to cultivate about one thousand acres of fair land lying between the mountain and the sea, while up its steep slopes vineyards are terraced by their labor, as was the custom in Palestine years ago.

Besides these there are many other persons in the land who, like Lady Stanhope, hold extreme or fanciful views on religious topics. Many Jews also find their way thither from Russia and other lands, under the hope that the ancient people of God will soon be restored to their beloved country and capital city. To this end societies have been organized, periodicals issued and explorers sent forward to inspect the country; but as yet no assured progress has been made, nor does it seem that the way is open for successful colonization at the present time.

With our one day's experience and observation we were quite willing to bid farewell to the little city by the sea; and as we had planned to leave the country at a northern port, it was our final adieu to Jaffa.

CHAPTER II.

SHARON AND RAMLEH.

Along the narrow lane, bordered by a stone fence, which leads up to the Mediterranean Hotel at Jaffa, we found our horses ready saddled for our afternoon's ride toward Jerusalem. If we had cherished any anticipations that we were to be mounted on fiery Arabian steeds, on which to give the natives an idea of an American's skill in horsemanship while passing through their country, the idea was quickly dispelled when we saw these animals. Not that the horses were poor or unsightly, but evidently they were not thorough-breds. We could not trace a single line in their build which bespoke the mettlesome charger. On the other hand, the whole group seemed very much at home in their present position, and as they stood along the sunny side of the wall, nodding sleepily, or resting their heads upon each other's haunches, we could not see that they differed much from the ordinary work-horses of America.

But, as has often been remarked, one cannot always trust to outward appearances; and some of our party, not exactly certain of their equestrian skill, were already casting longing eyes upon the more sleepy-looking animals, wishing that one of these might fall to them in the allotment. A horse in repose is quite a different thing from a horse in action; and who could tell what one of these peaceful-looking animals might do when he found a strange and an indifferent rider upon his back, as he snuffed his native mountain air on his way up to Jerusalem? All reflections upon the subject were cut short by the sudden appearance of the guide, who commanded all to mount and allotted the animal to be used by each rider. As it frequently turns out in human affairs, either the ambition to ride swiftly, or the fear of falling off, on the part of the riders, was not fully realized that day, but each traveller found enough to do in urging his horse onward in order to keep up with the party.

Beside our party of three Americans, we now had an English gentleman, Mr. H——, and Mr. Lemaitre, a young gentleman from Paris, mounted in company with us. An assistant guide, named John (of whom more hereafter), went before us in dashing style through the crowded little bazaar and led us out by the highway eastward. On either side the road was bordered by hedges of cactus or thorn, of luxuriant growth, behind which were the famous orange orchards. We could see the trees, now adorned with spring blossoms, while the green, the half-ripened and the great golden matured fruit hung upon the bending branches, or lay upon the ground ready for the hand of the gatherer. The oranges of Jaffa are the finest in Palestine and Syria. It is said that its pomegranates and watermelons are likewise in high repute, and its gardens and orange and citron groves are indeed fragrant at this season.

Having passed the orange groves, we soon came to the forks of the road, and just in the angle we found the structure which marks the supposed site of the tomb of Dorcas. According to tradition this is the place where the miracle was wrought by Peter restoring the good woman to life while the lamentations were in progress previous to her funeral.* The building is of fair size, one story in height, and is ornamented with three small domes and two small minarets. An arch, enclosing a sort of niche, adorns the otherwise solid masonry of the front, and is flanked by a twin window on either side. Tall and graceful cedar trees, on either side of the tomb, lend their solemn shade and heighten the beauty of the

---

* Acts 9 : 36–43.

TRADITIONAL TOMB OF DORCAS, AT JAFFA.

place. It seems fitting that this remarkably benevolent woman, whose good works were honored by her own people and have been commemorated by thousands of Christian societies in later ages, should thus have her tomb on this beautiful plain of Sharon. The fruits of holy living which she exemplified were grander, to be sure, than the grain and fruits of this fertile plain; yet the latter may be taken as a symbol of the former, so that there is a harmony between the tomb and its surroundings.

The very air was fragrant with the scent of orange and citron blossoms, wafted to us from the gardens we had just passed; and this we could not help regarding as illustrating in a certain sense the sweet memory of Dorcas.

Our guide now directed us to take the right-hand road, passing by the left which runs directly to Lydda, whence Peter came on his way to Joppa. We were now on the main thoroughfare to Jerusalem, a road broad and smooth, and evidently kept in repair for the accommodation of tourists and pilgrims. The fields on either side, while they were destitute of fences, appeared fresh and green, as might be expected at this season. The growing crops were chiefly wheat and barley, the former of a good healthful hue, but slow of development, and the latter "in the head," lacking but few weeks of the harvest. The soil appeared fertile, but no great proportion of it was under tillage; and here and there herds of cattle and flocks of sheep could be seen in charge of their keepers.

The general aspect of the country was not unlike the appearance of some of our prairie lands west of the Mississippi. One exception, and only one, occurred to us in passing, and that was the contrast in the people and the arrangement of their dwellings. In the far West the traveller will notice the cabins of the settlers sprinkled about here and there upon their claims and sections; but along the highway in ancient Sharon no trace of farm buildings was visible. Where do these farmers and shepherds have their dwellings? The guide pointed to the hills of Philistia looming up on our right, and informed us that for the sake of security the people lived in little hamlets at a distance from the highway. We could now distinguish their dwellings in groups perched up against the distant hillsides.

As we moved forward at an easy pace the fragment of an old hymn, endeared to all from childhood's memory, spontaneously suggested itself—

> "How sweet the breath beneath the hill
> Of Sharon's dewy rose."

We were on the lookout for one of these roses, but found not a single specimen. Osborn says that from ancient times the rose has been the symbol of beauty and of loveliness, and nowhere is it valued more than in the East. Some of the most pleasing and charming varieties grow on the borders of the Mediterranean; but the double roses, or at least the varieties, are seldom or never seen wild. He thinks that the famous roses of Sharon and Jericho were developed by cultivation. Dr. Thomson suggests that the rose of Sharon was a species of the mallow, and others think it a narcissus. We saw a number of brilliant flowers on the plain, but they were mainly poppies and anemones; could either of them have been the successor of the famous rose of Sharon, to which our Lord is likened in the Canticle? (2 : 1).

The clatter of a horse's hoofs upon the smooth, hard roadbed behind us put our musings suddenly to flight. The rider, whoever he might be, was coming on at a furious pace. Even our sleepy and steady-going animals were thrown out of their sedateness somewhat, and began shying and prancing in a manner quite terrifying to the uninitiated among us. So many stories have been related by travellers of the raids of the Bedawin upon tourists in the Holy Land that we might have been excusable for thinking that they were even now upon us. The fears of the timid, if any were in fear, were quickly dispelled by the sudden appearance of our guide in chief, whom we had left behind in Jaffa, mounted upon a coal-black charger and spurring past us, almost with the fleetness of the wind, and with a shout challenging us for a race. This was the custom of the land, we learned subsequently. Sheikhs, herdsmen, guides and muleteers are all fond of this exercise, and even the donkey boy, when allowed to hold a horse for a half hour, is quite certain to vault into the saddle and set off on a canter.

After this incident the whole party moved forward at a quickened pace, and at five o'clock we reached the village of Ramleh. We had now made twelve miles of our journey, averaging four miles to the hour, and this was considered a quick trip in this country. As we were to pass the night at this place in order that we might start at an early hour on the morrow for Jerusalem, we were taken at once to the ancient tower, which is regarded as the object of greatest interest. Dismounting at the foot of the tower, we gave our horses in charge of the attendants and began to inspect the ruins. We found ourselves in the midst of a large quadrangular enclosure, in every part of which were to be seen the fragments of

TOWER AT ER-RAMLEH.

what was once solid masonry. Here we saw the traces of former arches and walls braced by crumbling buttresses, while underneath were extensive subterranean vaults, still resting secure on their former foundations. It is supposed that these are the remains of what was once a splendid khan, where travellers halted on their journeys. Opinion is divided as to who were the original builders of all this masonry. Dr. Robinson, who investigated the historic evidences very fully, inclines to the view that the ruin is wholly Saracenic. This is in opposition to the traditional view which has always regarded this place as a relic of the former building of the Crusaders.

The tower, a great column of masonry, which stands like a grim sentinel keeping watch over the ruins at its base, is over one hundred feet in height, and is still in a fair state of preservation. It is evidently of Saracenic architecture, and stands towards the northwest part of the enclosure. It is square in structure, built of well-hewn stones, and its corners are supported by tall, slender buttresses. The walls taper upward by several stories to the top; and while the windows are of various forms, they all have pointed arches. The tower, Dr. Robinson thinks, was originally a minaret—a lofty structure used by the Mohammedans at the present day in many cities, from the top of which a sentinel calls out the hour when the faithful are to pray. He finds that it was erected by an Egyptian khalif named Muhammed Ibn Kalâwûn, about 1310 A.D., and required eight years for its completion.

We found the ascent of the tower quite fatiguing. Passing through the arched portal we began our task of climbing up the spiral stone staircase, in which we counted one hundred and twenty steps, each nearly a foot in height. As we reached each successive landing we caught, through the open windows, glimpses of the beautiful landscape around.

A charming view greeted our sight when we had reached the summit. To the northwest we had the extensive plain of Sharon stretched out before us. The surface of the plain was undulating, and the promising fields of wheat and barley, with here and there green meadows and pasture-land interspersed, gave abundant evidence of rich fertility. We noticed the minarets and domes of the large village of Lydda, about three miles distant, surrounded with its olive orchards and cactus hedges. Turning to the westward we traced the road by which we had approached the place, and in the distance caught sight of the bright waters of the Mediterranean. To the southward lay the hills of Philistia, already mentioned, studded with the little hamlets of the farmers, thus affording the choice feature of every beautiful landscape, the evidence of human habitation. To the eastward were the lofty hills of Judea, over which we were to make our way on the morrow. The rays of the declining sun lighted up the clearly-defined summits, while the narrow valleys were wrapt in the sombre shadows of the coming darkness; and at our feet, nestled against the base of this ancient and beautiful tower, lay the modern village of Ramleh, with its groves of olive trees and its luxuriant hedges of cactus.

Enjoyable as was this scene, the lateness of the hour warned us that it was time for us to descend, and cautiously feeling our way down the broken stone steps we soon emerged into the quadrangle and mounted our horses for the ride to our quarters in the village. This part of the day's journey was quickly accomplished; for in a few minutes we turned up one of the little streets and came upon a house with a flag floating from a staff planted on the roof, on which were the welcome words "Frank Hotel." The building had evidently been used formerly as a dwelling, but was now improvised for a lodging place for travellers. Its former owner was a Mohammedan, and here it was said he kept his harem. The lower story was now used as a dining-room and kitchen, while above were our lodging-rooms, opening out upon a broad stone terrace. Our evening meal was soon prepared, and served upon a very primitive table constructed of benches and heavy deal plank, while sacks of barley and other grain were piled in heaps against the heavy stone walls and in the gloomy corners of the basement room which served as our dining apartment. At an early hour we retired to our sleeping-rooms, nothing daunted by the thought that this was once occupied by the aforesaid harem; and, weary with the novel experiences of the day, we fell into our first sleep in Palestine.

CHAPTER III.

GOING UP TO JERUSALEM.

"Garçon! Garçon!! Garçon!!!" These were the words which rang through our ears like the blare of a trumpet, at daybreak on the following morning at Ramleh. We recognized the voice as that of our English fellow-traveller. With a feeling of alarm we hastily made our toilet and opened the door, fearing that mischief might be brewing.

Inn, or Khan.

We found our friend Mr. H—— standing in his open doorway, clad only as if he had just arisen from sleep, shivering in the crisp morning air, attempting to arouse the attendants in the basement. "Garçon" is the French name for waiter, and we concluded that Mr. H—— had adopted it, because we were now at the Frank Hotel, where French would seem to be most appropriate. We found out afterwards, however, that it was our friend's habit, when travelling in any foreign country, to make a dash at French, even if the people understood English perfectly well. "Garçon" seemed more polite and courteous than "waiter," hence, no doubt, its frequent use.

At last one of the guides appeared, whereupon a colloquy took place of a most animated description. It seems that Mr. H—— had determined that his luggage, consisting of several heavy trunks, should be kept with us during our month's journey. On this point a long debate had taken place at Jaffa, the guide wishing the trunks sent by steamer to Beirut, to await our arrival. A compromise had been effected by hiring an extra mule to transport the effects, and now Mr. H—— had awakened, in fear, lest his bundle of twelve canes and nearly as many umbrellas had been forgotten at Jaffa. Hence the alarm;—and what, with the mixture of fair English, bad French, and barbarous Arabic; the opening of the heavy mule packs, the braying of the animals, and the presence of wondering natives;—there was commotion like that in the baggage train of a great army. At last the particular package was found, just where it had been safely stowed away at Jaffa. Peace and order having been restored, the cook welcomed us to the breakfast table.

The sun was fairly above the high Judean hills when we mounted our horses to go up to Jerusalem. We wound around the cactus hedges, and high plastered walls enclosing the fine gardens of Ramleh, until, presently, we emerged into the open country. The soil here is of a sandy nature, yet very fertile; the village is surrounded by olive groves, while here and there an occasional carob, sycamore, or palm tree might be seen along the wayside.

A city was founded here by the Mohammedans in the early part of the eighth century, under the name which it now bears, Ramleh—"The Sandy." When the crusaders came, they captured it and made it one of their strongholds, in connection with Lydda and Jaffa. Here they celebrated a festival to St. George upon the abundance of provisions left behind by the fleeing inhabitants, and made the hero, who slew the dragon, their patron saint. To this day, England acknowledges St. George, and still raises the white banner with the red cross.

As we emerged from the narrow streets, and our little party straggled along the highway eastward, we thought of the contrast between our own appearance and that of the royal knights of ancient times. Richard Cœur de Lion may have swept along this road, with his magnificent army of crusaders, mounted on war-horses, their lances, shields, and battle-axes glistening, like mirrors, in the sun. Our steeds seemed entirely oblivious of the fact that they were on ground distinguished by such grand equine exploits. The only ambition they manifested was, a seeming desire, that each one should be last in the train, and we had much ado to urge them forward at a gentle trot.

In two hours we ascended the first foot-hill of the Judean range, and reached a miserable hamlet named *El-kubab*, situated on a rise of ground to our right. The guide informed us that the town formerly bore a very bad reputation; for not many years ago, a few gentlemen having some valuable goods in charge, while passing it in the night, were set upon and robbed by the inhabitants. When complaint was made to the Turkish officials they, in contrast with their usual indifference, placed the whole population under arrest, and confiscated all their cattle, sheep and grain, and by their severity taught the *Kubabians* such a lesson that they no longer seek for plunder, and are almost afraid even to ask for *backshish*.*

An hour later we reached the *Bab el Wady*, "gate of the glen," which from ancient times has been the chief entrance to the Judean range from the west. The descent into the valley of Ajalon is here quite steep, and thus nature has made it a place of defence. From this point we had a fine view of the valley and heights beyond. The vale of Ajalon is wide and fertile, and runs from northeast to southwest, having a stream-bed in its centre, through which the heights around Gibeon are drained. To the southward, in Philistia, David probably selected his pebbles from the bed of this water-course, when he fought his famous battle with Goliath.† Far toward the northeast, the guide pointed out the pass of Beth-horon, from which Joshua commanded the sun and the moon to stand still.‡ With the aid of the glass we were enabled to distinguish the town of upper Beth-horon, as the sun shone upon it through a rift in the clouds. It lay high up among the mountains, beyond the pass through which the discomfited Amorites must have fled

---

* This is the Arabic word for "present." Dr. Robinson spells it "bakhshish," Dr. Thomson has "buksheesh," and Canon Tristram, "backshish."

† 1 Samuel 17 : 40.

‡ Joshua 10 : 12.

away in terror into this valley of Ajalon, on the day of their utter defeat.

Near our point of observation is the village of *Latrŭn*, named thus from the tradition that *Disma*, the penitent thief, formerly was a bandit at this place. Lying in wait behind these high rocks on either side of the "gate of the glen," he would fall upon some hapless traveller and despoil him of his goods. Here also, it is said, is the native place of the famous Maccabees, who maintained a long and successful struggle with the Syrian kings, and finally succeeded in establishing, for a period, the independence of the Jews. About the year 175 B.C., on this very hill-top, Apelles, one of the Greek commissioners sent by Epiphanes, set up an altar for idol-worship, and commanded the people to offer sacrifices upon it. Only one poor Jew obeyed; when Mattathias, the priest, with his five sons appeared on the scene, putting Apelles and the Jew to the sword, and scattered the crowd of idolaters. One of the old priest's sons, named Judas—who is sometimes called the Washington of Judea—became the leader of the Jewish forces, and from these rocky hills, by sorties, and night attacks, and deeds of desperate daring, drove off the Syrians from the land.

At this point we began the toilsome ascent of

Kuryet el Enab (Kirjath-jearim).

the Judean mountains,—for mountains they are, though we are not accustomed to speak of them by this title. They are composed of a limestone of yellowish color. No forest trees, and but little grass or shrubbery, are found upon their rounded sides or lofty summits. Following the tortuous track of the highway, and gradually attaining higher and yet higher elevations, we came, near midday, to Kirjath-jearim. It was here that the sacred ark of the covenant abode for twenty years, after it was restored to the Jews. It had been taken to the battle-field by Hophni and Phinehas, the two ingrate sons of good old Eli, that it might be a charm to discomfit the Philistines; but, alas! the Philistines triumphed, and took the ark, with all the spoil, to their own land; whence by a providence they returned it, drawn in a rude cart by two new milk cows, to its proper owners.[*]

Few of the touching stories of Old-Testament history have a pathos equal to the story of that sacred ark. It came from the foot of Sinai, with the tables of the law. The history of God's dealings with his ancient people, the incidents in the lives of Moses, Joshua, Eli and Samuel, were bound up with it; and here on this sunny mountain slope, after it came from the great temple of

[*] 1 Samuel 6 : 7–12.

Dagon at Ashdod—after it was sent away from Gath, Ekron and Beth-shemesh—came this holy ark to the house of Eleazar the son of Amminadab, and here it rested until King David, with great pomp and a royal procession, took it up to Mount Zion.*

As we approached Kirjath-jearim, a cloud which had been hanging over the horizon in the south-west for some time, suddenly assumed a very dark and threatening aspect. A coming storm, the proverb says, hastens the traveller on his way; and our party, following the example of the guide, urged the horses into a quick pace down the hill, toward the little *khan* where we were to partake of luncheon. As I could not leave that place with only a passing glance, I rode under a fine olive tree by the wayside, just opposite the village, and waited till the storm should be over. I did not have long to wait: a gust of wind, a dash of rain, and the rattle of a brief hail-storm was upon me, and was soon past me, driving over the hills around Jerusalem. It was the last touch of the rainy season, and we did not see another drop of rain fall during the four weeks which we spent in Palestine and Syria.

The little village now looked quite cleanly and

* 2 Samuel 6.

inviting, as it had been washed by the passing shower. It lies on the eastern side of one of the high Judean hills, and not far from the summit which we had crossed only a few moments before. Its situation is at the edge of one of the peculiar bowl-shaped depressions which form such a characteristic feature of this mountain landscape. But while most of these upland vales have bare rock for their sides, this one is a terrace of fertile soil, occupied with fruit trees, vineyards and gardens; hence its modern name, *Kuryet el Enab*—"village of vines." It was a suitable place for the repose of the sacred ark, half hidden as it is in the shadow of the mountain, and surrounded with abundance of vines, olive and fig trees. The single-story stone houses with twin windows, with a fine old gothic ruin in front said to have been erected by the Crusaders and dedicated to the Knights of St. John: a mosque, a fountain, and the remains of an ancient khan enshrine this smiling hamlet as a pleasing picture in the memory. The extended prospect in front,—reaching quite across the vale of Hanina to the high hills before Jerusalem, with variety of mountain peaks guarding the deep wadies between, with here and there an orchard of olive or of fig trees set in the terraced hillsides,—affords the village of vines a suitable environment. Kirjath-jearim, the name by which we know this place in Old-Testament history, is truly one of nature's sanctuaries, and well deserves the honor of keeping, for twenty years, the sacred ark of the covenant.*

The traces of the shower had nearly disappeared when, a few minutes later, I joined the party at the khan in the valley, where we were to partake of luncheon. The khan of Palestine is neither a hotel nor a private dwelling. It is simply a shelter by the wayside where the traveller may rest, while he entertains himself with his own provisions, and, if he remain over night, may lie down upon his own bedding. The khans vary in size and in finish according to the location. On the long routes from Cairo to Damascus, or from either of these cities to Mecca, the buildings are of large size; but in the present instance the place was small and used as a dwelling, and the accommodations were very meagre. The structure was made of common field stone, plastered with clay, and the roof was made of sticks covered with brush and turf. An old man seemed to have the place in charge, and opened

---

* Robinson's map, "Environs of Jerusalem," locates Kirjath-jearim at Kuryet el Enab, but Conder and Dr. Chaplin propose Soba as its site, and the Palestine Memoirs suggest Khurbet 'Erma. The first two places are within sight of each other, so that the above description will afford the reader a view of the general surroundings in either case.

the door of welcome to us, upon the payment of a few piastres.

The guide, with his assistants, spread the cloths upon the ground floor, and brought forth the store of provisions; and as our appetites were good, after the morning's ride, we were anticipating a pleasant repast in this primitive hostelry. But scarcely were we seated around the edges of the cloth, after the Turkish fashion, before our troubles commenced. First came the chickens, half running, half flying across the place occupied by the dishes, picking at the bread, eggs, and meat as if they intended to make the most of this their golden opportunity. Following them came the cats, scarcely less persistent yet far more stealthy, and they nearly completed the work of destruction. It was indeed an embarrassing situation, and we soon despatched what provision each one had been fortunate enough to secure at the beginning, and prepared to retreat into the highway. Our hasty exit surprised a half-grown girl who had been watching us, with great black, greedy eyes, from the corner of the doorway. She would have made a good subject for any artist who could paint well from memory. She disappeared quickly around the corner of the building, her coarse black hair, and tattered tunic, streaming out behind her in the wind. We were unable to catch a glimpse of her afterward.

The khan had an elevated portion in the interior which extended over nearly one-half of the floor space. This raised portion was about two feet above the general level, and was composed of stone masonry, within which was a broad, shallow oven, securely arched at the top and covered with a coat of plaster. Upon this the bedding is usually placed during winter, so that, with a brisk fire of brushwood and dried grass kept up during the day, the people sleep in tolerable comfort at night, enjoying the heat retained in the stonework. In some cases the donkeys are kept upon the ground-floor, and the manger is placed along the front of the raised portion. Thus the ancient khan at Bethlehem must have been constructed with the cave in the rear, where, because there was no room for them at the inn, Mary wrapped the infant Jesus in swaddling-clothes and laid him in the manger.

Our route from the khan led over another hill of Judea, on the summit of which is a ruin named *Kustul*, an ancient fort of either the Romans or the Crusaders. High on the crest of the range to the northward we saw Mizpeh, the former tomb of Samuel, now named *Nebi-Samwil;* while, at an almost equal height and like situation, to the southward we saw a conical peak named *Soba*. As we advanced, these two summits were almost constantly in sight, and each seemed the more majestic and impressive the nearer we approached to them.

From Kustul we descended to *Kulonich*, which lies just on the border of the great valley Hanina. It is undoubtedly the site of an old Roman town, for near by it is a fine bridge of stone over the bed of the little brook, which shows the trace of Roman architecture. It is of interest to note that the little place named Kulonich, which is an attractive village, with gardens and vineyards surrounding it, is one of the supposed sites of Emmaus,[*] where the Saviour and the two disciples came on the evening of the day of his resurrection.[†] Could it be certainly proved that this is the very spot where that ever-memorable scene occurred, few places even in this most interesting land would be of greater interest to us. It is distant from Jerusalem just about the required sixty furlongs; and it is situated at the side of the ancient road leading westward to Kirjath-jearim and Ramleh, supposed by many to be ancient Arimathea. From Kulonich the

---

[*] Some authors locate Emmaus at Kubeibeh, farther to the north and west.
[†] Luke 24 : 13.

disciples could easily have returned the same evening, with their joyful tidings, to the holy city; and thus nearly all the conditions of the sacred narrative are met by this location.

From this point we crossed the arch of stonework already mentioned, and soon came to a high hill, which we climbed in a zigzag fashion by some eight diagonals, all included within a space of about one-fourth of a mile. It was in reality climbing up the face of a steep, and in places almost perpendicular cliff, and thus it formed a fitting climax to the fatigue of the day's travel. We were able from the top to gain a view along the winding track which we had followed from Kirjath-jearim, and also to take in the general appearance of the Judean hillsides. As a rule they are quite barren of vegetation. Slabs of limestone are seen all along their sides, glistening in the sunlight. The layers of rock are mainly horizontal, and swell in and out in curved lines around the projections and recesses, thus affording natural terraces, which once were under cultivation no doubt, but now are in a state of nature. In the beds of the deep, narrow valleys olive trees, and little gardens under cultivation, may be noticed; and higher up, in a few places, the natural terraces are occupied with vineyards.

While we were still among the mountains, as we supposed, we were almost at the gates of Jerusalem. Having gone a few yards from the summit of the cliff with the diagonals, we were already in the suburbs which lie without the city walls. We saw the upper and lower pools of Gihon, in the valley of Hinnom, on our right; and ere we could fairly realize it we were within the Jaffa Gate and dismounting in David Street, in front of the Mediterranean Hotel.

THE INTERIOR OF THE JAFFA GATE. (*After Photograph by Bonfils.*)

The Jaffa Gate, called also "Yafa Gate," "Hebron Gate," and by the Arabs *Bâb el-Khalil*, is on the west side of Jerusalem. It consists of a massive square tower, the entrance to which from without is on the northern side, and the exit within on the eastern. All the roads from the country south and west converge to this gate. One street—and it is generally the one first trodden by western pilgrims—leads from the Jaffa Gate eastward past the space by the citadel, and down the side of the ridge and across the valley to the principal entrance of the Haram. This street is called by some the "Street of David." Outside the Jaffa Gate is the usual camping-place of all travellers reaching Jerusalem by way of Jaffa and from Hebron or Bethlehem.

CHAPTER IV.

SIGHTS ON MOUNT MORIAH.

All readers of the Bible have, at least, a general conception of the surroundings of Jerusalem. And, in the main, the general view is quite correct, though the details will greatly vary from our ideal of the holy city. All have heard of the mountains round about Jerusalem, to which the Psalmist compares the watchfulness and care of Jehovah over his people. Even the stranger can find them at once, and without hesitation. Scopus, the Mount of Olives, the Mount of Offence, and the Hill of Evil Counsel are all in plain sight, and are easily identified. So also the two noted elevations within the city walls, Zion and Moriah, can be recognized at a glance; and even the valleys of Hinnom and Jehoshaphat have, at the very first sight, a familiar aspect.

If we were to remain without the walls we would not need a guide, except for his protection. We can walk entirely around the city walls within an hour,—only two and one-half miles in length,—and at first we feel disappointed that Jerusalem has only about twenty-five thousand inhabitants.

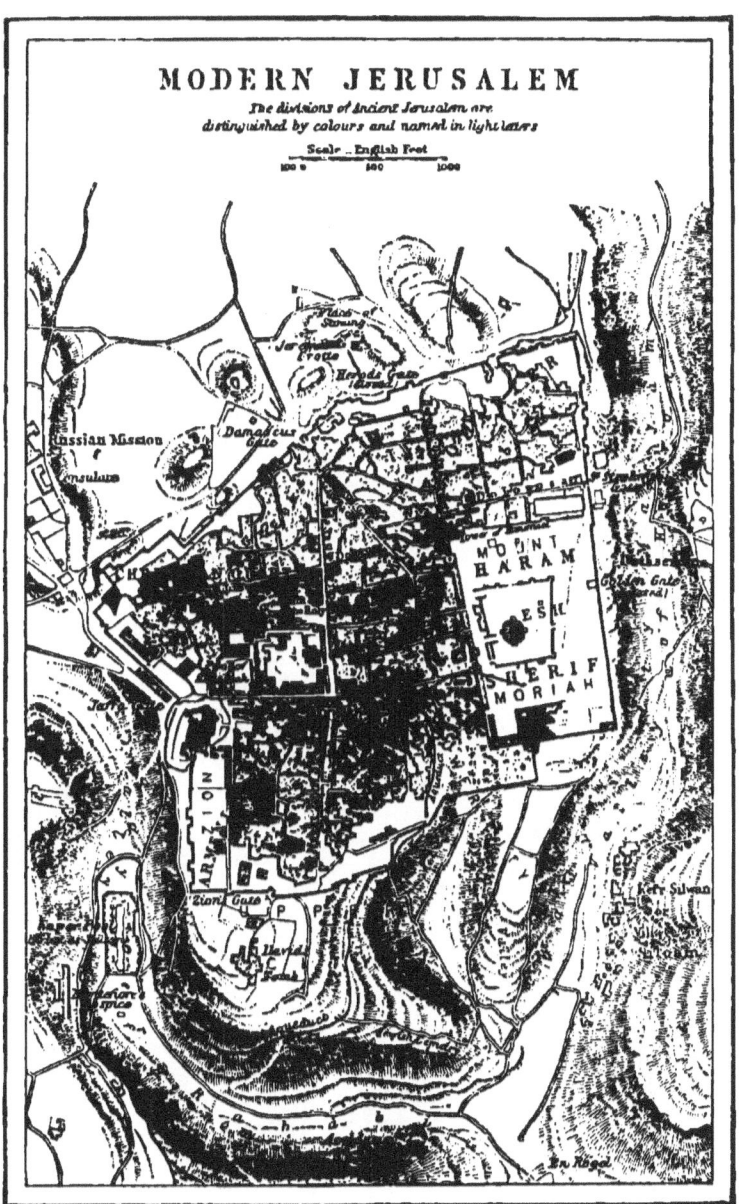

When we compare it with the cities of other countries, we at once discover that its greatness is not due to its size, nor to the magnificence of its buildings. There are at least one hundred cities in the United States larger, in population, than this famous city of the Jews. Yet we do not estimate the value of precious things according to bulk but according to quality, or to affection. Hence we must look at Jerusalem, not as a rival of other cities in population or wealth, but we must prize it for its memorable history and sacred associations.

It was with no ordinary interest that two members of our party took our first walk in Jerusalem, on the evening of the day of our arrival. As was most natural, our steps were directed towards the place where we could see the Mount of Olives and the Kedron Valley. With our guide we set out from near the Jaffa Gate, who led us down David Street, through the busy little market-place or bazaar. We found the streets not only narrow, but also very uneven and almost impassable, on account of the slippery condition of the surface. The pavement, in fact, was nothing more than a bed of field-stone of uneven surfaces, roughly laid down. Added to this was the difficulty occasioned by the fact that the streets follow the natural slopes in crossing the Tyropœon

Valley, and therefore are without anything like a smooth grade. The recent rains had covered the surface with a slippery coating of clay, and the little torrents were still at work carrying the mud, and debris, down the slopes in the middle of the streets. We had to use the greatest precaution, therefore, lest from an unguarded footstep we should find ourselves prostrate in some filthy puddle. At last, after turning this way and that, and by great care avoiding the loaded camels, mules, donkeys and high-stepping men, we arrived at St. Stephen's Gate. Passing through the gate we advanced a few paces, and stood upon the brink of the valley of Jehoshaphat. And now the view which we had so long desired to see was spread out to our anxious and scrutinizing gaze. At last we were permitted to see that of which we had read so often; of which we had studied, and thought, and dreamed.

The scene was as we had imagined, only the proportions were much enlarged. The valley before St. Stephen's Gate is broad and deep. In the bed of the valley there is room for extensive gardens at this point, and the space is enclosed and under cultivation. Gethsemane is also in plain sight, but it is quite a distance away, and, as now enclosed by a substantial wall, and well stocked with ancient olive and young cypress

THE MOSQUE OF OMAR AND THE HARAM AREA.

trees, it forms an attractive feature of this otherwise somewhat barren view. The Mount of Olives is high and broad; exceeding my anticipations in both particulars. The buildings on the summit, at this distance, appear to be quite new and large; but the broad face of the mount, lying between, looks bare and uninviting, save as relieved by the clumps of almond, fig, and orange trees which are scattered along the channels of the water-courses, and are already in the bud and leaf of the early spring. The feelings awakened by the sight were simply inexpressible, and for the most part we gazed upon it in silence; and, thoughtfully turning away, retraced our steps, waiting for views from other standpoints to give us a more accurate conception of the place as a whole.

On the morning following our arrival at Jerusalem we were taken to see the Mosque of Omar, which occupies very nearly the site of Solomon's temple, on Mount Moriah. The guide was anxious that this visit should be made at once, for the coming festivals, of both Christians and Mohammedans, would close the gates of the temple area against all sight-seeing tourists for many weeks to come. The *Haram esh-Sherif*, or Noble Sanctuary, is an elevated area five hundred and ten yards in length from north to south and three hundred and eighteen yards wide from east to west.* It is bounded by immense walls, the substructions of which are supposed to have been laid in the times of Solomon. The wall on the east side runs parallel with the valley of Jehoshaphat, and for a considerable part of the whole distance stands upon its very brink. On the west side the great wall runs along the narrow and now very shallow valley of the Tyropœon, in quite a similar manner; at the north end is the bed of an ancient cross-valley now known as the pool of Bethesda, and at the south the ground falls away rapidly over the rounded knoll formerly known as Ophel. The surface in the interior of this enclosed place, thus surrounded by valleys, has been levelled up by filling earth along the walls, until it now appears like a public square or park, shaded by cypress, olive and plane trees, with the celebrated Mosque of Omar situated well toward the western side.

This elevated section includes the entire summit of ancient Moriah, which David purchased from Araunah the Jebusite, and where, tradition asserts, Abraham offered Isaac for the sacrifice. And here Solomon erected his temple, which was

* The latest measurements are: west side, 536 yards; east side, 512 yards; north side, 348 yards; south side, 309 yards. This shows that the area is not an exact parallelogram.

afterwards restored by Zerubbabel, and finally enlarged and rebuilt in a more magnificent manner by Herod the Great. This spot, thus distinguished in sacred history, after the wars with the Romans finally fell into the possession of the Mohammedans; and here, it is said, the khalif Omar built the mosque (which still bears his name), in A.D. 686, occupying seven full years in its construction.

As our party approached this famous structure, our guide pointed out to us a smaller building at its side, not unlike an elegant summer-house in appearance, which was named Solomon's Tribunal or place of judgment. At the door of the great mosque we were required to remove our boots, but no restrictions are made respecting the wearing of hats, the Mohammedans themselves always entering their places of worship with the feet bare and the head covered. We found ourselves within an octagonal structure of elegant workmanship, fitly crowned by a graceful dome located exactly over the great rock which gives the Mohammedan name to the place—"The Dome of the Rock." Two rows of columns running quite around the interior of the building, of ancient appearance and finely polished, divided the area into two nearly equal parts. As usual, we found no pews within, for the Mohammedans either prostrate themselves, or sit upon the floor during their worship, and but few of the faithful were present at the time of our visit.

The sacred rock was the object of greatest interest to us. I had always formed the idea that it must be an immense boulder; but in this conception I soon found that I had been mistaken, for the sacred stone is simply a spur of the native limestone of Moriah, *in situ*, protruding above the floor of the sanctuary. It is in shape a sort of parallelogram, and is about sixty feet in length by twenty in width.* It appears to have been worked down with drill and chisel, the whole surface having thus been chipped away, leaving a slight comb or ridge its entire length from north to south. The guide pointed out to us the giant finger-marks made by the angel Gabriel when he grasped the sacred relic to prevent its following Mohammed up to Paradise. These were plainly nothing but drill-marks left in a convenient form to suit the legend.

Under the southern end of this rock there is the entrance to the cave or shallow recess beneath it. This portion of the sacred relic was

---

* Other writers give its length 57 feet, width 43 feet, height above pavement 6½ feet. The Mohammedans believe that at the last day the Ka'ba of Mecca will come to this rock, the blast of the trumpet will announce the judgment, and God's throne will then be placed upon this rock.

undoubtedly the projecting ledge of the original formation, under cover of which Araunah the Jebusite may have stored the wheat obtained from his threshing-floor near by.* Upon entering this cave, in which a dozen persons can gather and stand upright, we were shown the praying-places of David and Mohammed; and on stamping upon the floor, we found that it was hollow beneath. A large hole pierces through the projecting portion of the rock overhead, corresponding very nearly with the hollow place beneath, indicating that at some time there must have been some connection between them. The Mohammedans, however, will not allow any one to open the floor over the hollow-sounding place, alleging that the well of spirits lies below it, into which no mortal must penetrate.

Despite the usual shabby surroundings of all Mohammedan buildings, to which this is no exception, the Mosque of Omar is certainly a fine piece of architecture. The windows, located well up toward the eaves, are set in stained glass, without emblems, and are chaste and elegant in coloring and design. The capitals of the columns are finished in gold, and the walls are covered with mosaic work of an arabesque pattern. The mosque is not large, but is tastefully built, and

* 2 Samuel 24: 21.

the dome is graceful, symmetrical and a fitting crown to the whole structure.

We left the building by the southern portal, and noticed that the surface dropped down to a lower level, to which we descended by a broad flight of stone steps, and crossing a lawn of green sward, beneath which lie the numberless cisterns of the old temple area, we approached the second mosque, known as *el-Aksa*. We found that this was a larger building than the one we had just left, but it was not nearly as beautiful. Its southern end rests upon the great wall of the temple area, and from the windows on this side extensive views are enjoyed of the deep valley of Hinnom and its junction with the valley of Jehoshaphat at En Rogel.

Our guide next led us down a narrow and dangerous stone staircase into the vaults known as Solomon's Stables. There we found ourselves in a large subterranean apartment, filled with solid arches of masonry which evidently supported the floor and walls of the mosque above. At the same time we noted the immense stones imbedded in the foundation of the great wall at the southeast corner of the temple area. It was on the exterior side of this southeast corner of the ancient wall that Captain Warren sunk a shaft in 1868, and finally, after great labor and peril, found the corner-stone laid by Solomon's masons 2880 years before. "The corner-stone," he writes, "is let into the native rock apparently about two feet: it is well dressed, and has an

EASTERN WALL OF JERUSALEM AND MUSLIM TOMBS. (*After Photograph by Bonfils.*)

There are many cemeteries, sepulchres and tombs about Jerusalem, but the favorite burying-place of the Muslims is along the east wall, adjoining the *Haram esh-Sherif;* since, according to their traditions, the general judgment will take place in this locality. They say that all men will then assemble in the valley of Jehoshaphat (at the left of the picture). A thin wire rope will be stretched across the valley to the Mount of Olives. Christ will sit on the wall and Mohammed on the mount, as judges. All men must pass over the intervening space on the rope. The righteous will be kept by the angels from falling, while the wicked will be precipitated into the abyss of hell. Near the centre of the picture can be seen the Golden Gate, which has been kept closed from a very early period.

ordinary marginal draft of about four inches at the top. It shows above the rock about two feet." On a stone in the fifth course, and the second one from the angle, he found some characters marked with red paint, of which he writes: "The general impression resulting from the examination of these marks is that they are the quarry-marks, and were made before the stones were placed *in situ*. If this be the case, then the stones must have been dressed previously to their having been brought from the quarries." Thus the Scripture statement is confirmed: "And the house, when it was in building, was built of stone made ready before it was brought thither: so that there was neither hammer nor axe nor any tool of iron heard in the house, while it was in building."*

After ascending the stone steps which lead to the present surface of the temple area, we climbed to the top of the heavy wall which overhangs the valley of Jehoshaphat, and peered down into its awful depth. Captain Warren states that there is now about forty feet of soil in the bed of the Kedron at this point; so that originally the depth of the valley must have been increased to this extent. Solomon's Porch was built on the southern wall, of which Josephus says: "A broad portico ran along the wall, supported by four rows of columns, which divided it into three parts, thus forming a triple colonnade or portico. The height of the two external porticos was more than fifty feet, while that of the middle one was double, or more than a hundred feet. Such was the elevation of the middle portico above the adjacent valley that if from its roof one attempted

* 1 Kings 6:7.

to look down into the gulf below, his eyes became dark and dizzy before they could penetrate to the immense depth." Dr. Robinson estimates the depth of the valley at present as 150 feet, but thinks that from the middle portico it must have been 310 feet. At all events the depth is very great, and the visitor sees at once the force of the language in the Gospel which fixes a portion of the Saviour's temptation at this point, when "the devil taketh him up into the holy city, and setteth him on a pinnacle of the temple, and saith, If thou be the Son of God, cast thyself down."* Going on northward along the eastern wall, we soon came to the Golden Gate, which is now walled up with solid masonry. The double arch, with ornamental finish, may yet be seen, with the ancient lintel pierced for the reception of the standards belonging to the absent gates or doors. The Mohammedans have a tradition that when the Saviour's second advent takes place this gate will be reopened for the grand procession, and that then they will lose their possession of the holy city.

As we reached the northern wall of the temple enclosure we came to Birket-Israil, the traditional Pool of Bethesda.† It is an unsightly place, being

---

* Matthew 4:5.

† The Pool of Bethesda, near the sheep market or place, John 5:1-9, was identified with the modern pool *Birket-Israil* by Capt. Wilson (see *Recovery of Jerusalem*, pp. 148-156). This

TRADITIONAL POOL OF BETHESDA (*Birket-Israil*). (*After a Photograph by Bonfils.*)

was regarded as untenable by Barclay, as was also the so-called "Virgin Fount" (see *City of the Great King*, pp. 321, 325). He would identify Bethesda with one of the "two pools" named in the *Bordeaux Pilgrim*, one on the right and the other on the left of the temple. But Dr. Barclay supplies a supposed omission in the text of John 5 : 2, and confesses "there are no special vestiges of the pool to be seen at this time." Dr. Robinson proposed to identify Bethesda with the Virgin's Fount ('*Ain Umm ed Deraj*), above the Pool of Siloam (*Silwan*), and the Palestine Fund Exploration Report, just issued, adopts it, saying, "The modern Jews believe the waters of this pool to be a sure cure for rheumatic complaints. They often go in numbers, men and women together, and stand in their clothes in the pool, waiting for the water to rise. This fact, together with the meaning of the name Bethesda (house of the stream), renders it very probable that the Virgin's Fountain is the pool mentioned in John 5 : 2, which was near the 'sheep place,' possibly therefore outside Jerusalem." See *Survey of Western Palestine*, Jerusalem, p. 366; also Schaff's *Bible Dictionary*, arts. Bethesda and Jerusalem.—*Ed. Am. S. S. Union.*

partially filled with ashes and other rubbish, and without water. Captain Warren excavated this pool also, and found it to be the bed of an ancient valley, eighty feet in depth and running out into the Kedron. The pool was formed by constructing a wall along the sides and across this rock channel, and supplying it with water by a conduit. He found the depression to be thirty-five feet in depth, and thus was compelled to dig forty-five feet in order to reach the native rock at the bottom. This bottom he estimates to be 165 feet lower than the top of the platform around the Dome of the Rock.

In leaving this interesting enclosure we passed the site of the ancient tower of Antonia, which was located at its northwest angle. From Josephus we learn that around this tower the Jews rallied in their final conflict with the Romans under Titus, A.D. 70, for the possession of their sacred temple. The Romans were strongly entrenched in this massive tower, and the Jews, stationed on the temple platform, fought with the utmost desperation in their attempts to dislodge them. All their love and reverence for their sanctuary inspired the poor Jews, now reduced to the last extremity by famine and sword, with an almost superhuman heroism. It was their dying struggle for national existence; and the description of their historian is simply appalling, with its details of suffering, butchery, and frightful death. It was at this time, he alleges, that a poor Jewess slew her son, and was eating his flesh, to satisfy the pangs of hunger, when the Romans finally accomplished their overwhelming defeat, and broke into the portions of the city so long under siege. From this historical description we infer that Solomon's temple was situated toward the western side of the enclosure, and was connected with Antonia by a row of cloisters, which, being set on fire by the Romans, finally reached the temple and destroyed it.* Somewhere on the Noble Platform, as it is called, is the ancient temple site. The sacred rock must have been covered by it, and most likely was enclosed within the Holy of Holies, where the ark was kept. "In that dark receptacle," Dean Stanley writes, "two gigantic guardians were waiting to receive the ark, on the great day of dedication under Solomon. The two golden cherubs were spreading forth their wings to take the place of the diminutive figures which had crouched over it up to this time. On a rough unhewn projection of the rock, under this covering, the ark was thrust in, and placed lengthways on what is called the place of its

* Josephus: Wars, vi. 4, § 5.

rest."* The temple fronted the east, and in entering it by the Golden Gate, the worshipper came first into the Court of the Gentiles; thence by a flight of steps to that of the Jews, with the great altar of burnt offering and the brazen laver; and then, before him arose the beautiful sanctuary itself, constructed of marble and cedar-wood and ornamented with gold, having first the sanctuary with the altar of incense, table of show-bread and golden candlestick, and back of all, as we have seen, the Holy of Holies, which no man must enter but the high priest, and he only once in each year.

The ark had not reached its final rest, as the Jews fondly hoped, when it was thrust upon the projecting ledge of the sacred rock. Indeed this spot is as much a place of warfare as of worship. Four hundred years after the dedication of Solomon's temple, Nebuchadnezzar came,† "and burnt the house of God, and brake down the wall of Jerusalem, and burnt all the palaces with fire, and destroyed all the goodly vessels thereof." What scenes of strife and carnage have happened around the sacred rock from that time onward! The revolutions among the Jews themselves, the sieges of the Egyptians

* History of Jewish Church, vol. 2, p. 238.
† 2 Chronicles 36 : 19.

and Syrians, that of the Romans, the Mohammedans and the Crusaders, combine to make this one of the most bloody sites of human history, as it has for centuries been regarded as the most sacred.

Near the site of ancient Antonia runs the Via Dolorosa—Sorrowful Way—along which, tradition affirms, Jesus bore his cross to Calvary. This tradition is doubtless founded on the idea that the "common hall of the soldiers,"* mentioned by the evangelist, was located in this tower. This narrow street, beginning at St. Stephen's Gate, passes near the site of Antonia, and continues on a westward course until it reaches the bed of the Tyropœon Valley, when it turns southward along a street leading from the Damascus Gate for a short distance, when it again turns westward, and ends on the ridge behind the Church of the Holy Sepulchre.

On the Friday afternoon during our stay in Jerusalem we went to what is known as the "Wailing-place of the Jews." This place is on the west side of Mount Moriah, in the Tyropœon Valley, where the large bevelled-edge stones in the ancient wall indicate the substructions of the temple of Solomon. Thirty men and twenty women were present on that occasion to lament

* Matthew 27 : 27.

ECCE HOMO ARCH, VIA DOLOROSA.

over the loss of their temple and kiss the stones in the wall. The men read aloud in Hebrew

THE WAILING-PLACE OF THE JEWS.
(*From Photographs.*)

from a service-book, in a kind of chanting tone, while waving the body to and fro, and indulging in loud lamentations.

CHAPTER V.

TOUR TO HEBRON.

Having gone over Mount Moriah quite thoroughly, we thought it best to defer further examination of the holy city for the present and make a tour southward as far as Hebron. For this trip the arrangements had already been completed by our argus-eyed dragoman while we were exploring the temple mount. Accordingly we were early astir on Thursday morning, selecting our horses, strapping our water-proofs to the saddles, and consulting maps and guide-books.

On this occasion we were to have a new guide, named John Bornstein, the son of Moses. He was already on the scene of action in front of the Mediterranean Hotel, quite as enthusiastic as any of the party, and eager for departure. John was a native son of the soil, though of German descent. He was a mere stripling of some eighteen summers, with light-blue eyes and long auburn locks, and a certain reckless, rakish air about him that gave promise of high adventure. He was dressed in a mixed fashion, half European and half Arabic, with civilized coat and pants, a tarboosh on his head, and a broad belt at his waist gleaming with knife and pistol. With a gallant wave of the hand he exclaimed, "All ready now; will the gentlemen kindly mount?" This order, which came with the authority of a commander-in-chief, we instantly obeyed, and after a few clumsy hitches, the five of us found ourselves in the saddles, and with sundry flourishes on the part of our fresh steeds we made a dash for the grim old Jaffa Gate. Having safely passed the sleepy Turkish sentinel, who stood like a statue with his back braced against the "needle's eye," we came at once to the vale of Hinnom.

The banks of the ravine are rugged and quite steep here, and we were content to clamber down the declivity, without thought of further display of horsemanship, until we were safe at the bottom. The ascent of the southern bank was equally difficult, and each rider found sufficient employment in keeping his seat while the animals slowly clambered to the summit. At this point we found ourselves on the border of the plain of Rephaim, where in former times so many battles were fought between the Jews and the Philistines, in which King David played so prominent a part. For the first half hour we skirted along the eastern edge of this plain. It was without fences, but in part under cultivation, the soil apparently fertile and the surface thickly strewn with loose stones. It slopes gently to the southwest, and sends all its waters down toward the Mediterranean, even from the edge of the Hinnom, whose waters flow in the opposite direction to the Dead Sea.

Though we were upon the highway leading to the south country, and were almost within a stone's cast of the great metropolis of the whole land, yet we were following simply a winding path, marked out apparently by the footprints of the passing camels, horses, and donkeys. It seemed remarkable to Americans, that the people of this land had been content to follow this winding trail from the days of Abraham, with no other attempt at engineering than that accomplished by the feet of passing animals. Yet, strange as it seemed to us, we did not see a single wagon road in Judea, Samaria, or Galilee, except the indifferent one leading from Jaffa to Jerusalem.*

At the south end of the plain we ascended the slope of the hill leading up to the Greek convent named Mar-Elias. The buildings of this institution are quite new and attractive in appearance. They are finely situated on the highest elevation

---

*A diligence, or stage, runs from Beirut to Damascus; but this road is in northern Syria.

between Jerusalem and Bethlehem, and from this point the traveller can look upon the Mosque of Omar and the Church of the Nativity in Bethlehem; by a simple turn of the head he can see the birth-place of Jesus, the place where he taught in the temple, the site of Calvary, and the scene of his final ascension from the top of Olivet. And surely no place beside this can boast of such historical and sacred associations in its scenery, wherever the foot of man may find a resting-place the world around.

A smart canter, which seemed to be a piece of mischief on the part of our rollicking guide, who had taken this opportunity to test a new pair of spurs upon his steed, brought us quickly to a wayside structure which he called Rachel's Tomb. This was a small structure, not unlike a dwelling of that country in appearance. It consisted of two parts, on one of which was a low roof, perfectly flat, and upon the other was the usual dome found upon all the houses, but a little larger in proportion, as if intended to indicate that the building was used as a place of worship. And this we found was the case in fact, for the Mohammedans use this as a *kubbeh* or praying-place.* In their way they thus keep

---

* The kubbeh is a square building with a court on the east. The original building was open, with four arcades, one on each

up a standing testimony to the truth of the tradition that this is the veritable spot, "but a little way from Ephrath" (Bethlehem), where "Ra-

TOMB OF RACHEL, NEAR BETHLEHEM. (*After a Photograph.*)

side, supporting the dome. These have been filled in except on the east side, where a chamber has been added. The original building was 23 feet on each side, the arcades having a span of 11 feet. The height of the walls is 20 feet and of the dome 10 feet. A monument has been noted on this spot since A.D. 333. In A.D. 700 it is said there was a pyramid on the site, and also in A.D. 1100. In 1422 a Moslem building is noticed as standing on the place. The Palestine Survey states that "there is no reason to doubt the genuineness of the tradition in which Jew, Moslem and Christian agree." (See *Survey W. Palestine*, vol. 3, p. 130.)—*Ed. Am. S. S. Union.*

chel died, and was buried in the way."* This is but a poor memorial of a sad and touching event, but it serves to remind us that we are travelling in the footsteps of the patriarchs, and are upon the scene of one of Israel's heaviest sorrows. It is well that the beloved wife of Jacob is thus remembered, since the pillar erected by her husband upon her grave has long since disappeared.

As we were examining the place the sound of music fell upon our ears, and passing around to

EASTERN MOURNERS AT THE GRAVE.

the west side of the building we perceived that it was the wailing chant of some Arab women, who were sitting around the tombs in the adjacent grave-yard. Their song was a kind of monotonous

* Genesis 35 : 19.

chant, raised at intervals of a few minutes and then suffered to die away, as if the effort had relieved the overburdened heart of the mourners. Thursday of each week is devoted to this office on the part of women who have lately been bereaved of friends, and the custom seems to be quite prevalent throughout all Mohammedan countries.

We were reminded, while listening to this plaintive song, of the passage of Scripture which describes Rachel as weeping for her children, and would not be comforted because they were not.* The Scripture has been variously interpreted, but, in any event, we think that it must be referred to the slaughter of children by the order of Herod the Great, in and around Bethlehem, in order to cut off the infant Jesus from the hope of succession to the throne. And if Soba, five miles distant toward the northwest, be the Ramah named as the birth-place of Samuel, then the figure can be explained. Herod's slaughter of the innocents was horrible enough to cause Rachel to rise from this tomb and lament over the cruel death of her descendants, in which case her shrieks might be heard at Ramah, which is in plain sight of this place, though, as was said, some five miles distant. But, as for the Arab

* Matthew 2 : 18.

women, it seemed to us as if the children were there that day, weeping for poor Rachel.

Though we were now in sight of Bethlehem, we concluded to forego the pleasure of visiting it for the present, and, turning westward, pursued the more direct route towards Hebron. We were soon in the hill-country of Judea, and noticed the same features of landscape which we had observed in approaching Jerusalem from Joppa. On either hand were high hills, walled up with nature's masonry, the nearly horizontal strata running completely around the curved heads of the little valleys, and giving them a sombre and rather barren appearance. Not a tree or shrub appeared in sight. Loose fragments of stone were strewn along the crooked bridle path, and not a single house appeared along the rocky slope which lay between us and Bethlehem.

Coming to the summit of one of these wild and barren hills, our guide pointed to the valley stretching out before us, and announced that there lay the pools of Solomon. Another quarter of an hour brought us to the old Mohammedan fortress, now in ruins, located just at the side of the pools, originally intended for a khan, perhaps, to accommodate the caravans which might pass this way on their route from Egypt to Damascus.

The pools themselves were objects of great interest. They were originally built by Solomon for the purpose of supplying Jerusalem with water. Just at the base of the hill to the westward we visited the sealed fountain which supplies the reservoirs. A round structure, which may be compared to a low tower, built of stone, covers the fountain. By the light of a lantern we descended to the stream bed, and found a rivulet of pure water gurgling over the native rock on its way to the pools.

The pools consist of three reservoirs, lying one above another across the valley at higher levels as they approach the sealed fountain. They are built of squared stones, and bear marks of the highest antiquity, and are so situated that the bottom of the one is higher than the surface of the next below, rising one above another towards the west. They are all covered on the inside with a coat of cement, which must have certainly been renewed since the date of their original construction. They are of the following dimensions:

	Length.	Breadth (east end).	Breadth (west end).	Depth.
Upper pool, (160 ft. ab. middle pool.)	380 ft.	236 ft.	229 ft.	25 ft.
Middle pool, (248 ft. ab. lower pool.)	423 ft.	250 ft.	160 ft.	39 ft.
Lower pool,	582 ft.	207 ft.	148 ft.	50 ft.*

* Four springs are connected with the pools, one in a rock chamber, now closed by a wooden door. The water runs

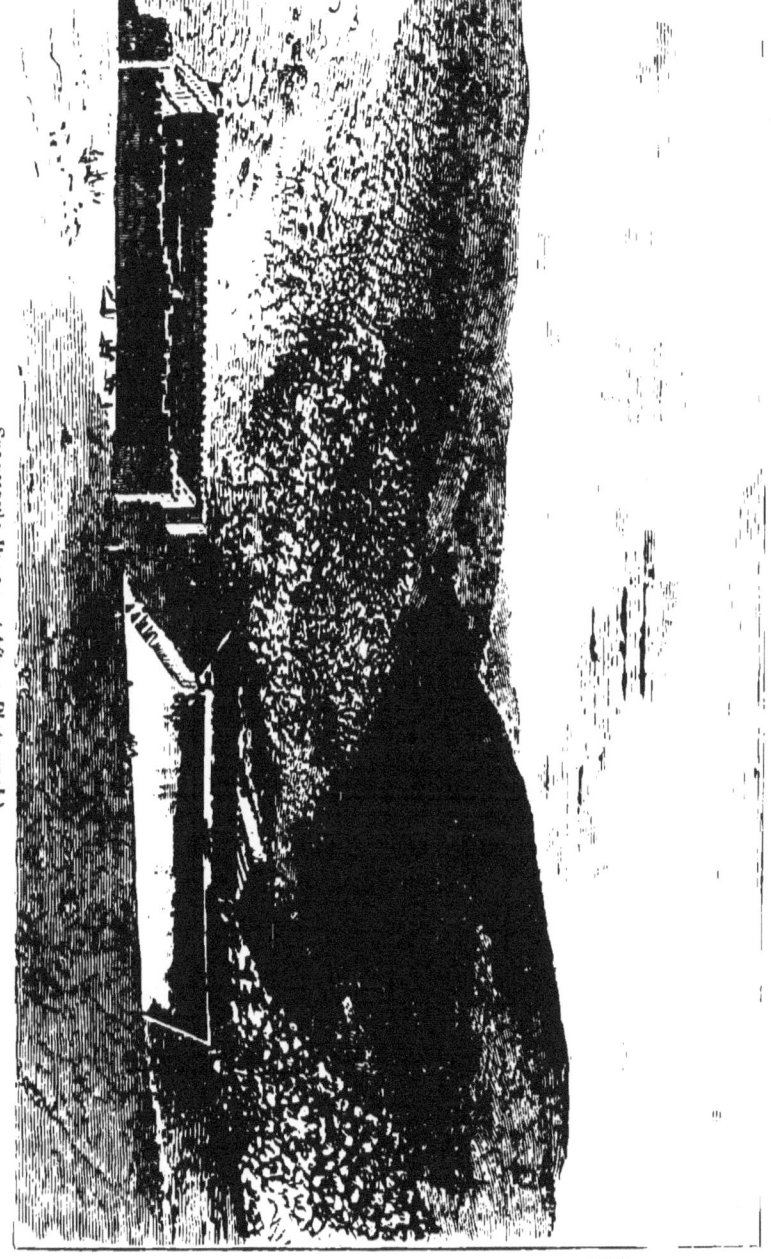

Solomon's Pools. (*After a Photograph.*)

Not far from these pools we came to quite a steep hill, over which the pathway ran in a serpentine manner, in order to avoid the masses of rock which projected their sharp edges into it, to the great discomfort of the passer by. We here met a large caravan of Hebron people on their way northward. Some were going up to Jerusalem, with their meagre stock of produce for the market, and others were pilgrims on their way to observe the feast of Moses, which was to be celebrated at his traditional tomb near Jericho. Some were mounted in a kind of basket on camels, others on donkeys, and still others went on foot. The party was composed of men, women, and children; the women carefully drawing down their vails at our approach, and the children peering over the baskets at us with wonder in their bright eyes, as they went swinging down the hillside, apparently without fear that the great camel on which they sat would make a misstep and dash them on the rocks.

From the summit of this hill we enjoyed another wide prospect. In a deep valley toward the east we noticed the remains of some ancient

through a vault into the west pool. A second spring is said to be beneath the pools; a third on the hillside southeast of the pools; a fourth inside the old castle north of the upper pool. The pools were further supplied from a well in the valley.—*Ed. Am. S. S. Union.*

stone structure, doubtless a ruined sheepfold, near which were some shepherds attending their flocks. The sheep were taller than those of our

EASTERN SHEEPFOLD.

own country, and nimbly skipped from terrace to terrace along the hillside, giving the shepherd enough to do to keep them together. They appeared to be constantly anxious to escape from him and climb up the steep hillside, and he was all the while on the watch to prevent them, for the best pasture was down at the foot of the hills and along the water-courses, where he was anxious they should feed. So, we thought, the Good Shepherd would keep us down in the humble vale, but we are ever anxious to climb up to some dangerous place of worldly distinction, where our souls would soon starve for the want of spiritual food.

"Oh, tell me, thou Life and Delight of my soul,
   Where the flock of thy pasture are feeding.
I seek thy protection, I need thy control,
   I would go where my Shepherd is leading.

"Oh, tell me the place where thy flock are at rest,
  Where the noontide will find them reposing;
The tempest now rages, my soul is distressed,
  And the pathway of peace I am losing.

"And why should I stray with the flocks of thy foes
  In the desert where now they are roving,
Where hunger and thirst, where contentions and woes
  And fierce conflicts their ruin are proving?

"Ah, when shall my woes and my wanderings cease,
  And the follies that fill me with weeping?
O Shepherd of Israel, restore me that peace
  Thou dost give to the flock thou art keeping!

"A voice from the Shepherd now bids me return
  By the way where the footprints are lying,
No longer to wander, no longer to mourn,
  And homeward my spirit is flying."

We now came into a delightful little valley, in the midst of which the waters of a brook made sweet music as it rippled over its shingly bed. Here we saw a profusion of wild flowers—pinks, buttercups, violets, wild tulips, anemones, and many others entirely new to us—which greatly heightened the beauty of the place. The music of the rivulet, the color and sweet odor of the flowers, with the song of the shepherds and the tinkling of the sheep-bells on the surrounding hillsides, made this a most delightful place.

Soon after we reached a little field of wheat in a widened part of the valley, where our guide began his usual pranks. No sooner had he reached the borders of the field, which was without any fence whatever, than he set spurs to his horse, and, shouting to us to come on, dashed through the midst of the growing grain. As we did not think it right thus to injure the farmer's crop, we kept along the border, but had to make great ado with whip and reins to keep him in sight, as he darted around the curves of the valley far in advance. When, after a thorough jolting, our knapsacks all in disorder, we overtook him, he explained to us that the farmers in that land thought it would bring good luck if a stranger would thus ride through their grain fields; and, as he was of an obliging disposition, he did not wish to pass through the country without doing all the good he could.

Leaving the pleasant little vale behind us, we next climbed another hillside, and found at the top one of the primitive threshing-floors so often mentioned in the Bible. It was located on the smooth rock surface, with a wall at the lower side, where the rock dipped beneath the soil. Of course it was not in use at the time of our visit; but in the harvest time the farmers bring hither the sheaves of grain, and drive the oxen over them until they tread out the kernels with their sharp hoofs. Then the straw is removed, and the grain and chaff are tossed up in the air that the wind may blow the chaff away. The grain, thus winnowed, is then removed to the dry cisterns for preservation, or to the farmer's house for future use.

While we were unable to witness the threshing process in Palestine, on account of the season of the year, we were gratified to see the process of ploughing and sowing, which was just then in

EASTERN PLOUGH.
[Similar to but not identical with that described.]

progress. In a little gravelly field against the hillside, not far from the threshing-floor, we came upon a group of men and boys just starting the plough. We dismounted and examined the utensil. The plough of Palestine is truly a primitive affair. It consists of an upright piece of wood, either a sapling or the limb of a tree, with a wrought-iron share, similar to the hoe of a grain-drill in shape, at the lower end, and a handle at the top. To this a horizontal piece of wood is fastened for a "beam," with a slim sapling lashed to its forward end, on either side of which the oxen walk as they draw in a long slender yoke. The plough could easily be lifted by one hand of the ploughman, and it only made a ripple in the soil, without turning a furrow. I counted fifteen men and boys in this group on the small field, with three yoke of little black oxen, and a camel and a donkey, for witnesses, near by. Our thrifty American farmers would be greatly amused at a sight like this.

Our lunching-place on this day was at a fine spring by the wayside, just at the foot of another long range of hills. Again we noticed the absence of dwelling-houses along the highway. We had not passed a single structure of the kind during our long ride from Jerusalem. But we now observed that the little hamlets of the farmers were located upon the crest of the hills, usually at quite a distance from the road. We could see two such hamlets from our present position. One, far towards the east, was named *Nebi-Yunis* (tomb of Jonah), and boasted of a sort of tower, erected in honor of the recreant prophet. At a nearer point, also on the hill-top, we saw the little village named *Hŭlhūl, i. e.*, praise (the Halhul of Josh. 15:58), and it is affirmed that it has borne this name for three thousand three hundred years. So little do the people in that land favor the progress which, many people think, comes with frequent alterations and changes.

As we rode up to the spring we found the place occupied by a single traveller, an Arab, evidently of some distinction, who was waiting while his splendid horse was drinking at the trough below the spring. He simply glanced at us with his keen black eyes, which flashed from beneath his white turban, in a half-inquisitive and half-defiant manner, as if he would question our right to the hospitality of the place. We thought that there might be some sort of collision between him and our mettlesome John; but the latter proceeded a little beyond the spring, and, dismounting, allowed his aid to hold our horses, while he set about the preparation of our repast. The Arab leisurely left the water-trough when his beast had satisfied his thirst, and, removing saddle and bridle, allowed him to wander at will, and crop the fresh grass which he found in abundance on every side. The horseman then spread his blanket and coat on the ground, and, bowing his head and pointing with his hands towards Mecca, began his prayers. He would kneel down, lie down flat upon his face, assume an erect posture again, all the while repeating something in an undertone. Nor did he give the slightest heed to his horse, or to the movements of our party, until his prayers were finished. Evidently this man was not ashamed of his religion, and we could but honor him for it, though we wished that he might come to know and worship that Saviour in whose land he dwelt.

Luncheon finished, we were again in the saddle, and, after making another tedious ascent, came upon the highest ground between Jerusalem and Hebron, where an ancient ruin lies eastward from the highway, named *Ramet* or *Beit el Khulil*, which we did not visit until our return. We now commenced our descent toward the valley where Hebron is situated, through the bed of a narrow ravine, where our horses found great difficulty in keeping a foothold because of loose rolling stones, which had been washed down by the late winter rains. From this narrow wady we soon emerged into the Hebron valley, running east and west, where, but a short distance in advance of us, we saw the dwellings and grand mosque of the ancient city.

Our entrance to Hebron was not calculated to inspire us with very exalted views of the place. We found the streets narrow and disgustingly filthy. The buildings were generally old and of inferior size, and rude in style of architecture. The inhabitants were either Jews or Mohammedans, and betrayed their ignorance and fanaticism in their manners and dress. As we alighted at the door of a kind of khan, where we were to leave our horses, a crowd of idlers leered at us insolently, and slunk away from our sight. The khan was a place for general repairs for both man and beast. It consisted of a large court-yard

View of Hebron from the South. (*After Photograph by Bonfils.*)

open to the sky, with stables at the farther side, while near the entrance was an arrangement which looked to us like a blacksmith's forge.

Having given our horses in charge of one of the attendants, our guide approached a grimy-looking man near the forge, whom we had supposed to be the smith, and said something to him in Arabic. Whatever was said, it seemed to have more influence with this man of swarthy skin, dirty hands and yellow, atrabiliary eyes, than we had supposed possible. He slowly arose from the round boulder on which he had been sitting by the side of the gate, and, going to the forge, raked together the fragments of charcoal smoldering there, and, taking an old tin vessel in his hand, proceeded to steep the black, thick coffee commonly used by the Turks. This, when prepared, he put with syrup into tiny cups, which may have been made of terra-cotta, but to us looked like lacquer-work from the coating of grease and soot. These cups the guide passed around to us with a lofty flourish, bidding us drink as an antidote for the fatigue of our long ride. We were too weary and thirsty to stand on ceremony, and so sipped the "villainous" mixture, which was like syrup for sweetness, and almost like lye for strength.

From the forge, which thus proved to be no forge at all, but a coffee-house, we proceeded on foot to inspect the Haram, or grand mosque. This large building, which stands just in the rear of the village, with its end thrust against the base of the steep hill overshadowing it, is supposed to cover the cave of Machpelah, which Abraham bought for a burial-place, and where, it is thought,

Abraham and Sarah, Isaac and Rebecca, Jacob and Leah are buried.*

MOSQUE AT HEBRON, COVERING THE CAVE AT MACHPELAH.

We were not allowed to enter the building, because we were not Mohammedans, and were led around to the hillside just back of the mosque, close to the wall where it is affirmed the cave is situated.† It has been thought that the body of

* Genesis 23 : 17–20.

† Only four times have Christians been permitted to enter this mosque—the Prince of Wales in 1862 and 1881, the Marquis of Bute in 1866, and the Crown Prince of Russia in 1869. The visitors were accompanied by Dean Stanley, Fergusson, Rosen and others. The Hebron Haram is almost an exact copy in miniature of the temple area at Jerusalem. For concise description of Hebron and the cave of Machpelah, see *Schaff"s Dictionary of the Bible*, pp. 372, 575, 576.—*Ed. Am. S. S. Union.*

Jacob, being embalmed by the skillful Egyptians, may be still in a good state of preservation; but the cave is regarded as so sacred that even the Mohammedans are not allowed to enter it, and thus nothing positive is known regarding its present contents. The tradition is probably correct, however, which locates Machpelah here, and we were not many feet away from the resting-place of the patriarchs. This in itself was a great privilege, and we could scarcely realize that Abraham had often looked upon this stony hillside against which we were standing, nay, that his feet had often rested on these enduring strata of limestone rock, which change not from age to age. But the best authorities affirm that the veritable Machpelah is located within the walls of the Haram, and there doubtless slumbers the dust of the ancient and illustrious dead. There lie

> "The patriarchs of the infant world, the kings,
> The powerful of the earth, the wise, the good,
> Fair forms and hoary seers of ages past—
> All in one mighty sepulchre."

There was little in Hebron to interest us, besides the site of the mosque and the general aspect of the surrounding hills. We returned to the khan without molestation, though assailed by fierce looks and threatening gestures from the rough men in the streets. We were prepared for all this by reports of previous travellers, but had not anticipated fully the fact that Hebron is one of the most secluded and out-of-the-way places of this unprogressive country. With no outlet of travel, except through the stony bed of a ravine, and a rough trail over the mountains to Jerusalem, twenty miles distant, these long-haired Jews, and ochre-colored Arabs of Hebron, will pass through the round of life, in this nineteenth century, with the idea that there is just one other nation besides themselves, namely, Franks, whose traders come to their town to gaze upon their mosque and rough hillsides. They will live and die in blissful ignorance of all the mighty seas, continents, and cities beyond them, and of all the improvements, inventions, and refinements of modern life, and also, it is to be feared, without a true knowledge of the way of salvation through the Redeemer.

In passing from the khan we came to the pool over which David hanged the murderers of Ishbosheth,* and, emerging from the town, passed on our way up the valley, westward, to the Russian hospice, where we were to pass the night. This is a large and well-built structure, located at the side of the great terebinth tree, known as Abraham's oak, on the north side of the pleasant

---

* 2 Samuel 4 : 12.

vale of Hebron. Before the sun had set we passed over on foot to the summit of the opposite hill, and took in an extensive view towards the desert. The great ridges of black rock swept away to the southward like the huge rolling billows of a mighty ocean, there transfixed and petrified. With the aid of the field-glass and the pocket compass and map we looked towards the site of Sodom, whence perchance from this very hill-top Abraham "gat up early in the morning to the place where he stood before the Lord," and saw that "the smoke of the country went up as the smoke of a furnace."*

Almost within sight, southward, lay Juttah, the birth-place of John the Baptist, and farther away to the southwest was Beer-sheba, another of the haunts, and homes, of the patriarchs.

Having thus taken in the wide barren landscape before us, we turned to examine the vineyard enclosure where we were standing. Never before had the description of the parables of Scripture been so fully realized. Here was the "hedge" around the outside to keep out intruders. Here was the "lodge" occupied by the vineyard dresser in the grape season, and at one corner was the "tower" from which he could look all over the place and detect the presence of an enemy.

* Genesis 19 : 27, 28.

Approaching twilight warned us to seek our hospice, and, with weariness, yet with delight and gratification at what we had seen, we re-crossed the beautiful valley to our lodging-place for the night. Upon our arrival the guide informed us that a good view of the whole valley could be had from the roof of the building, to which we at once ascended. There we saw the constellations come out in a radiancy never seen by us before or since. The air was so clear that Sirius appeared almost like the great sun which he really is. The mighty dome, radiant with beaming stars, seemed to span the narrow valley and rest upon the hill-tops on either side. The giant oak stretched out its long branches almost under our feet, where, it is said, Abraham and Sarah entertained the three angels. It was late at night before we retired to our rooms; nor will we soon forget our stay at Hebron.

CHAPTER VI.

FROM HEBRON TO BETHLEHEM.

With the early morning our indefatigable guide was astir, and when the sun first shone on the mosque of Hebron our little party filed through the narrow valley of Eshcol, lined with vineyards on either side, and took its way back towards Solomon's Pools, over the route by which we had passed on the preceding day. We had no good reasons for doubting the tradition which fixes upon this little vale as the Eshcol whence the spies brought the branch with one cluster of grapes, which they bore between two upon a staff; whence also they brought of the pomegranates, and of the figs.*

The fruitfulness of Eshcol has evidently not diminished since the times of the Exodus. Fine vineyards were to be seen on either side of the little wady, with low stone walls surrounding them, most of them also having a tower at the side or corner of the enclosure. At one time, by actual count, there were fifty-eight towers in

* Numbers 13 : 23,

VINEYARD IN SYRIA.

sight, most of them in good repair, though a portion of them were in partial ruin.

After ascending the hill we came in sight of the ruined village named *Khurbet en-Nusara* (*i. e.*, the destruction of Christians). Some years since the Mohammedans fell upon the Christians here, and either put them to death or drove them from the district. The whole region is now occupied by Jews and Mohammedans, and thus evidently Moslem fanaticism has reached a rank growth at Hebron and in its environments. Somewhat to

the eastward, and on a height of ground, we
found a slight depression of the surface, where
again our guide led us directly through a field
of growing wheat to an ancient ruin known as
Beit el Khulil. The remains of fine stone walls,
as of the foundations of several buildings, are
here plainly to be seen, covering an area of
about two hundred by one hundred and sixty
feet. The Jews call this ruin "the house of
Abraham," and claim that the shallow depression, extending in front of it from east to west,
is the true vale of Mamre. It is likely that
this is the ruin of a church begun by Constantine
the great builder about 320 A.D., but never completed.*

It was ten o'clock when we reached Solomon's
Pools once more; and as we were to meet with
another party of tourists, who had not yet arrived

---

* This *beit*, or house, is a very old ruin. It is called "Abraham's house," by Benjamin of Tudela, in the twelfth century, and is so called by modern Jews of Hebron. It is perhaps the market mentioned by Sozomen (Hist. ii. 4), where Hadrian sold Jewish captives, A.D. 135, and near Constantine's basilica at the terebinth of Mamre. Two courses of the house wall remain; one is 162 feet long, and the other 214 feet long, and each wall is 6 feet thick. A well a few feet from the west wall is called *Bir el Khulil*, "the well of the friend," *i. e.*, Abraham. The well is 17 feet in diameter, lined with ashlar cut carefully to the curve of the well. About fifty yards east of the *beit*, is the ruin of the basilica of Constantine. See *Survey of Palestine*, vol. iii. pp. 322, 323.—*Ed. Am. S. S. Union.*

from Jerusalem, we had ample leisure to survey all the surroundings of the place. We entered into the ruins of the old fortress or khan, and found traces of its former importance still remaining. The walls were from eighteen to twenty feet in height, enclosing a large quadrangle; and along the inside of the walls were huge ranks of earthen jars lying upon their sides with their mouths, or open tops, turned outward, and from these issued great numbers of bees in quest of honey. As the morning was warm and bright the honey makers were very busy, and the old khan was once again filled with nearly as great buzz and bustle as in days of yore, when pilgrims from Egypt and from Damascus passed in and out of the arched gateways.

The party from Jerusalem having arrived, we now set out for Bethlehem. Our course lay along the north side of the three pools, and then followed the line of the ancient conduit through which Solomon conveyed the water to Jerusalem, some eight miles distant.

Continuing eastward beside the valley *Urtas* we kept well up along the hillside, which was in places quite precipitous, with a grim gray surface of solid rock. The valley soon fell away into a deep bed, where we saw a little village with fertile gardens, the site no doubt of ancient Etam.

This may have been the scene of some of Samson's wonderful exploits.

And here also Solomon had "a garden and orchards, and planted in them of all kinds of fruits," and "pools of water to water therewith the wood that bringeth forth trees."*

And Josephus states that the king laid a causeway of black stone along the roads that led to Jerusalem, and that he used to go out of the city in the morning upon a chariot, attended by fine courtiers, dressed in a white garment. "There was a certain place, about fifty furlongs distant from Jerusalem, which is called Etham; very pleasant it is in fine gardens, and abounding in rivulets of water; thither did he use to go out in the morning, sitting on high in his chariot."†

The valley of *Urtas* could be conveniently watered from the sealed fountain and pools just above, and thus again be easily restored to its ancient fertility and beauty.

Soon after this we came to the eastern face of the mountain, and turning northward we reached the gardens and fig orchards surrounding Bethle-

---

* Eccl. 2 : 5, 6. This village is doubtless correctly located in the valley of Urtas. The *Palestine Survey* suggests that the name is retained in '*Ain* '*Atân*. It was near Bethlehem and Solomon's Gardens, and 50 stadia from Jerusalem. See *Palestine Survey*, vol. iii. p. 43.—*Ed. Am. S. S. Union.*

† Antiquities, viii. 7, §§ 3, 4.

hem; and urging our horses up a steep bridle-path we found ourselves upon the summit of the ridge, and in one of the narrow streets of the city honored as the birth-place of Jesus.

We made our way at once to the Latin monastery, and dined with the brothers at the refectory,

BETHLEHEM. (*From Original Photograph by Bonfils.*)

who showed us every attention after receiving the customary fee from the guide. From this building, which is a portion of the large structure known as the Church of the Nativity, we passed into the main portion of the edifice, and down into the apartment which is shown as the cave of the Nativity.

Here, it is said, the infant Jesus was born,

wrapped in swaddling-clothes, and laid in a manger.* There is every reason to believe that the tradition is correct which affirms that near this spot is the birth-place of the world's Redeemer. As early as the second century Justin mentions it, and in A.D. 325 the empress Helena began the foundations of the present edifice to mark and preserve the sacred site.

We found ourselves in an apartment some thirty-eight by eleven feet in size, with a flat ceiling of native rock about eight feet in height. On one side was an alcove, in the vaulted arch of which hung a number of silver lamps, which shed their mellow light upon a marble slab below. In the centre of this slab was set a large silver plate with star-shaped points on its circumference, and the words, "Hic de Virgine Maria Jesus Christus natus est," engraved upon it.

On the other side of the room we were shown the place where the manger stood, in which the infant Jesus was placed by his mother. Pilgrims were coming and going by the wide stone stairways at either end of the apartment, who, bowing low before the two sacred shrines, impassionately kissed and embraced the cold marble, meanwhile reciting their forms of service. One could not but follow their movements with interest, seeing

* Luke 2 : 7.

their profound earnestness, and recalling the facts here commemorated. Many of them had hoarded their meagre earnings for years, in their far-off Russian homes, and now they had devoted their all, to travelling and other expenses, for this joy of praying at the place of their Saviour's birth.

From this scene we were led by our guides, through a narrow passage, to the little grotto where Jerome passed some thirty years of his life in translating the Scriptures. And from this we returned by the same passage, and then ascended to the choir of the church, the altar of which is located just above the cave of the Nativity. Here also a service was in progress, and in a chapel at the side, a large number of women were engaged in their devotions. Conscious that this shrine worship must be liable to many defects, we still regarded the people as entirely sincere, in their devotions, at the birth-place of the world's Redeemer. Passing on, we soon completed the circuit of the holy places, and leaving the rambling structure, in which Romans, Greeks, and Armenians have their altars and cloisters, we came into the open air, and made our way to the eastern end of the hill on which Bethlehem stands; and upon which a village has stood from the days of Ruth and David, and probably from the time of the patriarchs. At this point we had our most satisfactory view of Bethlehem and its surroundings.

The town is situated upon a high narrow ridge, which extends eastward from the main hills of Judea, and has abrupt banks on either side. It has one main street near the crest, which is flanked by others of less pretension. The houses are built of stone, and are of a better class than those of Hebron, for the people here are prevailingly Christians. There are about five thousand inhabitants in the town, and the elevating character of their faith is noticeable in their dress, manners, and architecture; and yet in these respects there is opportunity for vast improvement. The houses are mainly grouped near the junction of the ridge with the main hill, and then spread out to a point just beyond the Church of the Nativity, where they fail altogether, and leave the extreme summit unoccupied. To this unoccupied place two of us made our way, and sitting down upon a rock enjoyed the beauty of the scene.

Looking westward we saw, on either side of the village, the terraced gardens, vineyards, and olive orchards, with neat division-fences built of the loose stone which lie in profusion on the surface surrounding them. The gardens, the village, and the crowning edifice from which we had just come, the centre and ornament of the whole, together made up a pleasing picture.

Looking eastward an extensive landscape opened before us. Over a vast region of country the eye wandered at will, and noted the historic places of biblical interest. In this plain just at our feet were the wheat fields in which Ruth gleaned in the days of Boaz.* Yonder in the far distance lie the fields of Moab, from whence she came on her long journey with Naomi. And there, just a little farther away than the fields of Boaz, like a shelf against the hillside, lie the fields where the shepherds were keeping watch over their flocks by night on the first Christmas eve :†

> "When such music sweet
> Their hearts and ears did greet,
> As never was by mortal fingers strook;
> Such music (as 'tis said)
> Before was never made,
> But when of old the sons of morning sung,
> While the Creator great
> His constellation set,
> And the well-balanced world on hinges hung."

It was the overture of the angels, "Glory to God in the highest, and on earth peace, good will toward men."

Turning the eye southward we look at the

---

* Ruth 2 : 2–17. † Luke 2 : 8–14.

rugged fields of Tekoa, where the herdsman Amos left his occupation to enter the list of the sacred prophets. And there is the dun-colored truncated cone, now known as the Frank Mountain, where of old the Amorites kindled their beacon fires, and where in later times Herod the Great had a palace, and where he made his costly sepulchre.

On either side of this ridge of Bethlehem little stream-beds are visible, which run out into deeper wadies, and these again into the *Urtas* and Kedron valleys. The ridge itself falls away by steps of immense magnitude to these ravines; and far away, across the gray and rounded hills of limestone, may be seen the deep, deep depression in which lie the bitter waters of the Dead Sea, and along its farther side extend the giant cliffs of Moab.

Once more, before leaving the place, we glance along the side of the ridge towards the cave of the Nativity. It must have opened northward toward Jerusalem, and as Joseph and Mary came up the steep ascent, after their toilsome journey from Nazareth, it offered them their first choice, and only available shelter.

One more mark of biblical interest we found in Bethlehem. It was the traditional well of David, to which the young men broke through the ranks of the Philistines, and brought of its water to the thirsty chieftain, who then poured it out on the ground as an offering.* The well is located on a hillock just without the gate on the roadside toward Jerusalem.† As we dismounted and peered down the face of its dark walls, we heard a sepulchral voice from within utter something in Arabic, at which we were at first startled, but were quickly reassured by the explanation of the guide that some men were at work making repairs in this well, which appeared to be rather a huge cistern. As we rode on toward the holy city we cast many a longing look backward at the crags and gulches behind us, where David as a shepherd boy fought his battles with bears and lions while in charge of his father Jesse's flocks and cattle. Presently we were at Rachel's tomb again, and, hastening our pace, we were not long in reaching Jerusalem.

* 1 Chronicles 11 : 17–19.
† The modern cistern or so-called "David's well" cannot certainly be identified with the true site of the well named in 2 Samuel 23 : 14–17. Tradition has identified it with cisterns a few minutes walk from Bethlehem, though the tradition is not much older than the fifteenth century.—*Ed. Am. S. S. Union.*

CHAPTER VII.

WALKS ABOUT ZION.

"Walk about Zion, and go round about her: tell the towers thereof. Mark ye well her bulwarks; . . . that ye may tell it to the generation following" (Psalm 48 : 12).

HAVING gone over Mount Moriah upon our first arrival at Jerusalem, we followed the advice of the Psalmist with respect to Mount Zion. The word "Zion" means "the sunny place," and doubtless this portion of the holy city was thus named because its slope faces the east and south, where the rays of the sun have their strongest

VIEW OF JERUSALEM FROM THE SOUTH.—Jerusalem covers four or five hill-summits. Within the city walls, on the southeast, is Mount Moriah, the site of the temple, now covered by the Haram enclosure or square, within which is the Mosque of Omar. West and southwest of this is Mount Zion, a portion of which is without the city wall. Directly south of Moriah is the hill Ophel, also without the wall. North of Mount Moriah is Bezetha, or the "new city," and west of Bezetha, in the northwest part of the city, is Akra. (Some, however, regard Akra as the northwest part of Mount Zion.) East of the city is the Kedron, or valley of Jehoshaphat. South of Mount Zion is the valley of Hinnom, which extends around on the west side of the city. The valleys of Hinnom and of the Kedron unite south of the city. Between Ophel and Mount Zion is the Tyropœon Valley. North of the city is Scopus, east of it the Mount of Olives, and on the south the Hill of Evil Counsel,

View of Jerusalem from the South. (See note, preceding page.)

influence. The ridge of Zion is a little higher than its near neighbor Moriah, and the shallow depression known as the Tyropœon Valley is all that separates them. The Zion ridge at its southern end overlooks the valley of Hinnom, from whence its eastern face runs northward until it reaches a point opposite the temple site, where it curves to the left hand, and continues until its traces are lost in the higher ground to the west.

The first object of interest on the southern shoulder of the mount, where once stood David's palace, is a vast pile of masonry, with turrets at the top and port-holes beneath them, known as the tower of David. It is an ancient and impressive piece of architecture, with hyssop growing out of its gaping seams, and, as it is connected with the high wall which entirely surrounds the city, it was only intended for defensive purposes. Near by this structure, which would be almost useless now in view of the methods of modern warfare, we visited the Armenian church, supposed to occupy the site of the palace of Caiaphas.

A gentle old priest of the Armenian faith conducted us through the little church, with its grotesque lamps, which are kept burning continually. and displayed an old Bible and other relics, such as paintings, tapestry and "the petrified blood of St. James."

Near by we were taken to the upper chamber in which tradition says Jesus instituted his supper on the night of his betrayal. We found ourselves in a large, but dingy, apartment, controlled by the Mohammedans, and kept by them as a sort of holy place. The walls were in an untidy condition, having been at some remote period covered with a lime-wash, which was now deeply weather-stained and uninviting in appearance. The ceiling was sustained by three groined arches, which rested for their support upon three pillars near the centre of the apartment. The entire aspect of the place was forbidding, and can only be viewed by Christians with dissatisfaction. There is small ground for believing it to be the room where Jesus and his disciples observed his last passover.

In the rear of this chamber we were shown the traditional tomb of David, in which we observed a huge sarcophagus, twelve feet in length and broad in proportion, covered with Arabic signs after the style of the royal caskets at Constantinople. Upon returning from this spot we were shown a place in the court-yard of the Armenian buildings where, it is claimed, the apostle Peter stood when he denied his Master. We next re-

Tomb of David. (*After a Photograph by Good.*)

turned to David's Street, which begins at the Jaffa Gate, and runs eastward past the tower of David, the Mediterranean Hotel and the quarters of the American legation. It is for the most part narrow, poorly paved and untidy to the last degree. It passes between the pool of Hezekiah and the Jewish quarter, and then enters the little bazaar, through which, by a sharp turn to the left, the visitor may reach the Church of the Holy Sepulchre. In following this route the tourist has been walking along the eastern face or slope of Zion, and finds at least that the Church of the Holy Sepulchre is located in a place where the configuration of the ground favors the view that it was anciently a garden.

Those who hold to the traditional theory affirm that Joseph's garden may very well have been at this point, and the "new tomb" could have been

POOL OF HEZEKIAH, INSIDE THE JAFFA GATE. (*After a Photograph by Bonfils.*)

conveniently excavated in the side of the limestone ridge, while near by might have been the knoll named Calvary.

The one passage of Scripture, however, which is urged against the theory that the Church of the Holy Sepulchre, which is located just on this face of Zion, well towards its upper or western end, covers the exact spot occupied by the cross and sepulchre is that "Jesus suffered without the gate."* The gate, of course, was in a line with the city wall, and at present the wall is outside the location named, and therefore it is inferred by some writers that this site is simply traditional,

* Hebrews 13 : 12.

and cannot be regarded as the true location. Others answer that at the time of the Saviour's crucifixion, and burial, the city wall ran from a point near the junction of David's Street and the bazaar, directly towards the Damascus Gate, northward, and thus was within the place now covered by the church and its associated structures.

Besides this, it is affirmed that constant tradition from the time of the empress Helena, who first began the work of erecting a chapel here, through her son Constantine the Great, has fixed upon this place as the true site of the cross and sepulchre. The question is far from a satisfactory settlement.

The external appearance of the Church of the Holy Sepulchre is not very impressive. From the large open court on its eastern front it appears as a vast pile of ancient masonry, about three hundred and fifty feet in length by about two hundred and eighty in width. Two square towers, with flat tops, and a broad arched entrance in the middle are the most prominent features.

Upon entering, the visitor finds himself in a large central auditorium, in the middle of which is the marble chapel or mausoleum, covering the sacred sepulchre, and around which are the private chapels of the Latin, Greek, and Armenian churches. The mausoleum itself is divided into two small compartments, in the first of which the window is shown through which the holy fire is handed out on the occasion of the Easter festival. The second compartment is the most sacred of all, for it is said to contain the rock of the true sepulchre, though this is carefully concealed under a slab of pure white marble. Forty-four beautiful lamps hang above this marble sarcophagus. Three paintings cover the walls, the central one with a portrait of the Saviour, with the scene of the resurrection at one end, and one of the ascension at the other. Only four or five persons can be admitted to the place at once, for it is scarcely more than six feet square, and, as may be supposed, the air is close and almost stifling by reason of the presence of this procession of pilgrims, who follow each other within to kiss the marble and pray before the paintings.

Upon leaving this consecrated spot we were taken to a room located quite in the rear of the great auditorium, and evidently along the low cliff of ancient Zion, where we saw the traditional tombs of Nicodemus and Joseph of Arimathea. These open tombs were side by side, cut out of the soft yellow limestone, and, as Dean Stanley has well observed, are evidently very ancient, and therefore give proof that this was once indeed a place

INTERIOR OF THE CHURCH OF THE HOLY SEPULCHRE.

of burial. Various other relics were displayed to us afterward in different parts of the building, and finally we were taken up a flight of steps to the traditional site of Calvary. This rock was likewise covered with marble, and a silver star, pierced with an orifice about two and one-half inches in diameter, indicated the place where the cross stood, and near by a crevice was pointed out which was held to be a trace of the rending of the rocks at the crucifixion.

We were favored with a view of the great ceremonies held in this place at the Easter season by attending service on Palm Sunday, under the escort of Colonel Wilson, the resident consul of our government in the holy city. Early in the morning we undertook to make our way through the crowd at the church door by the aid of Turkish soldiers. At last we pressed our way in, and obtained seats in one of the balconies which overlook the vast amphitheatre, surrounding the sacred mausoleum.

Soon after we had taken our places a stir in the crowd announced the approach of the first procession. It proved to be the Latins (Roman Catholics), and was composed of a company of priests, chanting as they marched, attended by persons bearing elegant smoking censers. Then came boys with banners, followed by the higher dignitaries, all dressed in sacerdotal robes, attended also by men with smoking censers. Here followed monks and others bearing palm branches, which they waved in the air. After marching three times around the sepulchre they halted at the entrance, and performed a brief mass, and then, under the conduct of Turkish soldiers, they retired to their own chapel.

Soon afterwards the procession of Greeks entered from their private chapel, followed by their patriarch, grandly attired. They had louder singing, finer banners, a greater profusion of decorated palm branches and a larger procession. They marched three times slowly around the place, and ended their service, as the Latins had done, with a mass at the entrance to the tomb.

Finally the Armenians appeared, with a greater number of participants, with still more gorgeous robes, with louder singing and a greater concourse of people following. They paused when halfway around the third time, and formed a circle of their priests, while the patriarch was seated in his great ornamented chair. Then boys came with beautiful fresh flowers, pink and white, and scattered them in profusion on the pavement before them. At last they finished their service as the others had done, and, amid great enthusiasm on the part of the spectators, withdrew.

We had occupied our places in the little gallery from seven until eleven o'clock in the forenoon, and were glad to regain the open air and street, apart from the surging crowd, where we could reflect more calmly upon what we had seen, and realize that, if we were not on the very spot where the cross and the sepulchre were located, we were at least not very far from it. In this, as in other instances, we found more satisfaction in examining the general topography and surroundings of the so-called holy place than in the "inventions of men" respecting it.

CHAPTER VIII.

OLIVET AND BETHANY.

Next in interest to Moriah and Zion, we turn toward the Mount of Olives. One morning our guide appeared again with the horses before the Mediterranean Hotel, and when our little party were mounted, proceeded through the Jaffa Gate, down the vale of Hinnom, on the way to Olivet and Bethany. Though it was only the 5th of April, the rays of the sun fell fiercely upon us in this valley, where the perpetually-burning fires of Gehenna used to remind the Jews of perdition. Here too stood Molech, the brazen idol heated within, where the fanatical among them used to sacrifice their children.*

At En-rogel, the junction of the two valleys, we paused to look upon the place where Solomon once had his magnificent gardens, a spot now barren and unsightly. A number of lepers' houses are crouched along the foot of the Mount of Offence, while just above on the Kedron is the poor village of Siloam. The base of the hills, and the bed of the valley, were alike destitute of

* 2 Kings 23 : 10.

tree or verdure, while the gray rock around gave no intimation that such fertility was once there, as must have been within the gardens of Solomon

POOL OF SILOAM.

In passing up the bed of the Kedron we dismounted at the pool of Siloam, and penetrating the dark interior beneath the broken arch obtained a cup-full of the tepid water, of which every tourist loyally partook, but with many a grimace of countenance and shrug of the shoulder, for the wash-women had given the water a strong flavor of soap-suds that day. From "cool Siloam's shady rill," as the poet expresses it, we passed on below the southeast corner of the temple wall, and on the other side of the Kedron dismounted again to visit the tombs of Zacharias, St. James, Absalom and Jehoshaphat.* We found nothing very remarkable

ABSALOM'S TOMB. (*From Original Photographs. Bonfils.*)

* The *tomb*, or as it is usually called the *pyramid of Zacharias*, was erected, according to tradition, in memory of the Zacharias of Matt. 23 : 35; 2 Chron. 24 : 20. The pyramid resembles "Absalom's Pillar," only it is not as high, being about 29 feet. The *tomb* or *grotto of St. James* consists of several small underground chambers, cut out of the rock. The entrance is through a long narrow passage. Tradition says that St. James the Great was concealed here after the crucifixion of Christ, and ate no food until the resurrection, and that St. James was buried here, though another tradition says his sepulchre is on the Mount of Olives. The *tomb* or *pillar of Absalom* stands in a heap of rubbish, and is about 47 feet high. It is called *Absalom's Pillar* from

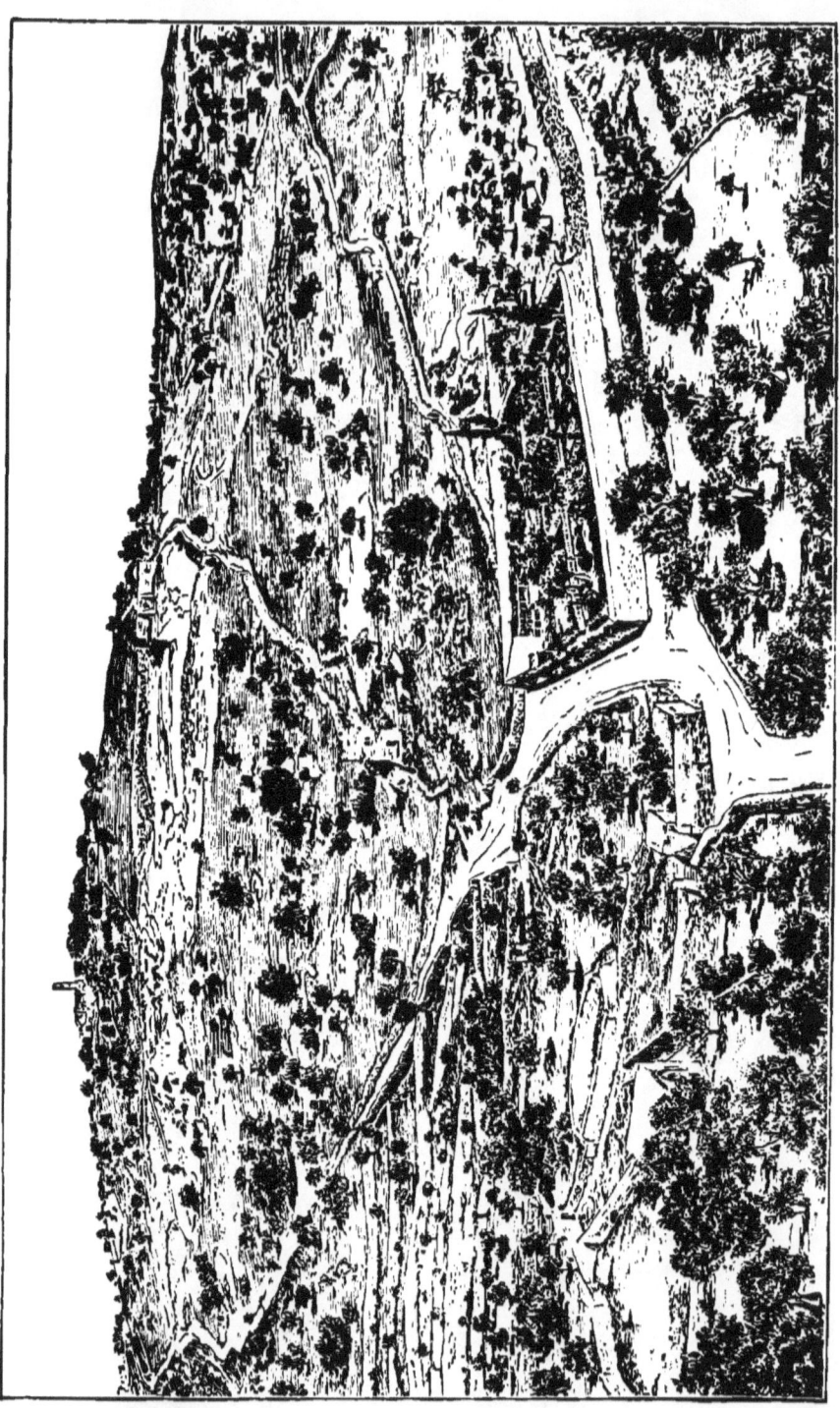

MOUNT OF OLIVES.

about these tombs; but noticed that one of them was cut out of the native rock, and we also noticed that on both sides of the valley, wherever there was room, tombs and graves had been located. When passing away we noticed a group of boys and young men, evidently of Jewish extraction, in the act of throwing stones against the tomb of Absalom, thus evincing their hatred and contempt for his character as of old.

The garden of Gethsemane was next visited, situated on the slope of Olivet, near the Kedron and opposite St. Stephen's Gate. The garden at present is enclosed with a high wall, the entrance to which is by a low doorway on the east side, so constructed that the visitor must stoop very low in order to enter it. This, we thought, a very remarkable and yet fitting expedient to teach all comers to that sacred spot the lesson of humility and reverence. The priests of the Latin Church, who have the garden in charge, have laid out the ground into neatly-kept parterres of flowers, to which the ancient olive and cypress trees in the centre add dignity and grace. The attendants showed us polite attention, and upon

its supposed identity with that mentioned in 2 Sam. 18 : 18. But there is no mention of it before A.D. 353, and the present is a comparatively modern structure, probably of the Greco-Roman period.—*Ed. Am. S. S. Union.*

our departure presented each one of us with a choice bouquet of cut flowers.*

From Gethsemane we followed the main road towards Bethany and the Jordan, and as we turned the curve around the southern shoulder of Olivet, where the level stratum of limestone rock forms the road-bed, we paused and reflected that Christ surely was near this spot when he wept over Jerusalem.† At this point, in his approach from Bethany, the view of the temple and the city would suddenly burst upon his sight.

In continuing this route to Bethany, we found that a ravine on this side of Olivet caused a sharp curve of the road northward to a suitable crossing-place, after which the way ran southward again so far that we could see the southern portion of Zion, but could not see the temple mount. At the extremity of this second spur of Olivet our guide pointed out several tombs or vaults, to which there were graded steps for descent, and said that this was the site of Bethphage, but of this assertion gave us no certain proof.

Shortly after we reached Bethany, and found it a small group of poor dwellings situated near

---

* For detailed description of size of garden, the walls, the olive trees and objects of interest, see Schaff's *Dictionary of the Bible*, p. 332.

† Luke 19.: 41.

the base of one of the long low ridges on the eastern side of Olivet. Here are about twenty families without thrift or industry. The ruin of

BETHANY. (*After Photographs.*)

an old dwelling, built of coarse masonry, is named the house of Martha and Mary, while at another place is shown the tomb of Lazarus.* Here again we fell in with a large company of pilgrims belonging to the Greek Church, who were performing their usual shrine worship. In our turn we descended to the bottom of the "sepulchre,"

* The tomb of Lazarus has been shown in Bethany since the fourth century, when a church stood over it. The tomb is now shown northeast of the "castle of Lazarus," in a vault reached by twenty-six steps. It is probably the site of a subterranean chapel of early date. The tomb was formerly shown in the church above.—*Ed. Am. S. S. Union.*

which we found to be a straight shaft sunk perpendicularly to the depth of twenty-five feet, having a spiral stone staircase within, upon which the pilgrims were ascending and descending, while panting for breath on account of the excessive heat of the place. At the bottom we noticed only a tiny altar with the usual tinsel upon it, before which the pilgrims bowed and prayed and then hastily departed.

The name "Bethany," as is well known, signifies the House of Dates; but we saw only a few almond and fig trees in the gardens, and could not find a single palm tree remaining to confirm the ancient title of the village. It is now called *El-'Azariyeh,* in allusion to the death and resurrection of Lazarus. The identity of the place is generally conceded, and its distance from Jerusalem, just two miles, and its relation to the Mount of Olives, fully confirm this view. Here indeed is Bethany, but how changed since the days when Jesus tarried here at the welcome home of the sisters of Lazarus!

> "And this is Bethany; and here abode
> The favored family whom Jesus loved;
> To whose warm, humble welcome 'twas his wont,
> Tracking the path that now I passed along,
> Oft to retire from foes and wavering friends."

We now resumed the saddle again, and climbed

the eastern slope, to the Church of the Ascension, on the top of Olivet. From this point we obtained a fine view of the entire city, of Scopus and the valley of Jehoshaphat on the north, and of Bethlehem, the Frank Mountain and the hills of Judea on the south, and of the Jordan Valley and the Dead Sea on the east. The sun was now near his setting, and his departing rays shed a soft radiance over the landscape, and as we stood there, near the place where "Jesus lifted up his hands and blessed his disciples, and was parted from them and carried into heaven," we could not help thinking that the scene is worthy of even that great event.*

Standing here on the day of his ascension, with one glance of his eye Jesus could see the place of his human birth and death. Bethlehem and Calvary are both in sight, and Zion and Moriah, the home of the ancient prophets, priests and kings, the temples and palaces of the holy city, all were there just before him, as if ready to lay their final, crowning tribute at his feet. While contemplating the earthly settings of this grand and solemn event, the words recorded by the beloved physician came up to our recollections: "Why stand ye gazing up into heaven? This same Jesus, which is taken up from you into

* Acts 1 : 9.

heaven, shall so come in like manner as ye have seen him go into heaven."*

We prepared to descend the western slope of Olivet by the path which runs furthest northward, now well worn by the water-courses, and the passage of the pilgrims of the centuries, since the days when Jesus passed this way, and hastened past Gethsemane to our shelter for the night. As we passed into the gate of St. Stephen the full moon arose upon the summit of Olivet, and reminded us that this was indeed the anniversary week of the Saviour's passion, death, and glorious resurrection from the dead.

One evening, during the same week, we were invited to attend the celebration of the Passover in one of the Jewish dwellings on Mount Zion. The gentleman who acted as our escort was an acquaintance of the family, and had obtained permission previously for our visit. We set out from David's Street, near the bazaar, our friend preceding us with his lantern—there are no street lights in Jerusalem—and penetrated that curious labyrinth of lanes and courts known as the Jewish Quarter. Our route was both angular and circuitous, sometimes leading up by steps from one plane to a higher, and anon descending by another flight to a lower level. The houses on

* Acts 1 : 11.

either side were lighted up in honor of the feast, and the farther we went the greater evidence of festivity appeared. At last our escort stopped before a door at the left, and holding the lantern in one hand rapped upon the panels with the other. While thus waiting for a response we could not help thinking of Hunt's celebrated painting of a figure of our Saviour standing thus, lantern in hand, before the door of a vine-clad cottage, with the title engraved beneath, "Behold, I stand at the door and knock."*

In response to the summons of our conductor the door was opened, and we were cordially received by the inmates, who were now prepared to begin the feast. Along one side of the large family-room a row of seats had been extemporized for our accommodation, while on the other side the members of the household were about seating themselves at the little table, upon which were a dish of green herbs, a shoulder of roast lamb, some eighteen loaves of unleavened bread and a decanter of wine.

The ceremony began in an informal way, each member of the family first washing the hands, and then taking a sip of the wine. A bright lad, of some ten years, then read from a Hebrew service-book as to the nature of the feast. After

* Revelation 3:20.

this a bag containing a loaf of the unleavened bread was held upon the shoulder of the different participants in turn, and bitter herbs were dipped in a kind of sauce, and then passed to us visitors that we might taste of the mixture. As it would be discourteous to refuse, we did partake, under a severe mental protest, however, and afterward this protest was strengthened by a recollection of the nauseous taste, and the woody fibre of the plants used in the preparation of the dish. After this, another section of the service was read describing the plagues of Egypt, the mere mention of which tainted the unleavened bread to such an extent that a little wine was poured into a dish with water, and set out of doors for purification.

After this came a season of pleasant intercourse, in which the old grandmother, and even the little babe in its mother's arms, united with great glee; the wine was passed around (not to visitors), the unleavened bread broken, and another long section of the Exodus read.

As the hour was late, and there seemed to be no near prospects of closing the feast, our party with many an obeisance and hearty salaam took leave, and returned by the same conduct, and lantern, safely to the Mediterranean Hotel.

CHAPTER IX.

TOUR TO MIZPEH AND GIBEON.

Our party was favored in having horses in readiness whenever we wished to make excursions to the environs of Jerusalem, otherwise a great deal of time would have been consumed and much fatigue experienced. In going out to the tombs of the Judges, and *Neby Samwil*, we again took to the saddle. The morning was bright and clear, and the air bracing. Again we went out of the Jaffa Gate through an extemporized market, which some peasants had organized on the bank of the Hinnom.

On the skirts of this quondam market we noted several lepers from the lazar-houses near *En Rogel*, blear-eyed, scorbutic and muffled up in rags, clamoring and wailing for *backshish*. Beyond this we passed along the row of shops, where mementos of olive wood are manufactured and sold by the German colonists, who have quite a large suburb here without the city walls, and are engaged in this trade for subsistence.

Continuing in a northwesterly direction we soon came to the tombs of the Judges. These are located in the face of a cliff with exposure to the north, being about two miles from the city. The range of hills from these tombs eastward is

Tomb of the Judges. (*From Photograph by Good.*)

named Scopus, from which a fine view of Jerusalem may be obtained, and where many armies have been encamped, during sieges or attacks, in the many wars which have been waged around the holy city. The tombs are simply a cavern cut into the soft rock, separated into different rooms, the walls of which are prepared with fifty-nine receptacles for the dead. These crypts are entirely vacant, and the doors leading from one room to another are open. It is said that this is the most remarkable of the catacombs around Jerusalem, since the crypts are arranged in three stories, the upper stories with ledges in front to give convenient access, and to support the stones that close them; the whole so essentially Jewish that it might be of any age, if it were not for its distance from the town, and its architectural character. By the fine pediment, wrought out on the face of the cliff, many writers pronounce the tomb a piece of Greek architecture rather than Jewish.*

Beyond this point we found that the ground sloped westward toward the vale of Hanina. The whole surface was covered with loose stones, with apparently little attempt at cultivation. As we proceeded, the lofty peak of *Neby Samwil*, our immediate point of destination, became more and more distinct, and at last, after a toilsome ascent

---

* The tombs of the Judges have been known to the Jews since the Middle Ages as the *tombs of the Sanhedrin*. The internal arrangements are peculiar. There are seven *kokim* at ground level on the north wall of the first chamber, and over these are *arcosolia*, each with two *kokim* at the back. There are two inner chambers on the east at different levels, containing *kokim* in two tiers; on the south a chamber with *kokim* and *arcosolia* above them, this chamber being also at a different level. Over the outward door is a richly rock-cut Grecian pediment of debased style. Within the vestibule a very richly-executed doorway leads into the main room, containing thirteen loculi in two tiers as above stated. Another door opens from this main room to a second room on the same story having nine repositories or loculi. In the northeast corner of the main room is a stairway leading down to a room beneath, the last mentioned and containing ten or twelve loculi, and in the southwest corner of the main room is a stairway leading down into an unfinished apartment. There are sixty loculi, while the Sanhedrin had seventy-three members. See *Survey of Palestine*, vol. Jerusalem, p. 407, and *City of the Great King*, p. 186—*Ed. Am. S. S. Union.*

of its rugged sides, we reached the miserable hamlet perched upon its summit.

As we halted at the edge of the town all the children came rushing upon us, calling out, "Backshish! backshish!" and actually fighting with each other for the privilege of holding our horses. As there were a great many more children than horses, the strife among them was very vigorous, in some cases resulting in blows, the girls apparently having the best of it.

After this warm reception we walked to the old tower, or mosque, named "the tomb of Samuel." It is at present in a ruinous condition, and we had no difficulty in entering it and ascending its flat roof and minaret, from which an extensive view is had of the surrounding country. The building was once a Latin church, Dr. Robinson thinks, built upon older foundations in the form of a Latin cross, and probably dates from the time of the Crusades.*

Of the beauty and extent of the view from

---

* The tradition which points to *Neby Samwil* as the birthplace, residence, and burial-place of the prophet Samuel is without proper foundation. The church which now covers the reputed tomb was finished in 1157 A.D. Numerous Hebrew inscriptions are written on the plaster of the walls, but they are quite modern. This site was recognized as the tomb of Samuel in the sixteenth century, but had been declared to be a false site by Benjamin of Tudela in the twelfth century.—*Ed. Am. S. S. Union.*

this place Dean Stanley says: "Of all points of interest about Jerusalem none perhaps gains so much from an actual visit to Palestine, as the lofty peaked eminence which fills up the northwest corner of the table-land, seen in every direction, the highest elevation in the whole country south of Hermon, commanding a view far wider than that of Olivet, inasmuch as it includes the western plain and Mediterranean Sea on one side, as well as Olivet and Jerusalem in the distance, backed by the range of Moab." The old Crusaders came this way, by the pass of Beth-horon, as they went up to capture the Holy Sepulchre and city. "It is a very fair and delicious place," says Mandeville, "and it is called Mount Joy, because it gives joy to pilgrims' hearts; for from that place men first see Jerusalem." Richard Cœur de Lion probably stood on *Neby Samwil* as he first beheld Jerusalem; when "he buried his face in his armor with the noble exclamation, 'Ah! Lord God, I pray that I may never see the holy city, if so be that I may not rescue it from the hands of thine enemies!'"

Not the least interesting object in sight of the observer on *Neby Samwil* is the broad mound near its base, on which is situated the little group of houses known as *el Jib*. This is the ancient Gibeon, without doubt, which figures so prominently in the historical books of the Old Testament. And if so, then this *Neby Samwil* is surely ancient Mizpeh,* watch-tower, and it is also the "high place" to which Samuel was about to repair from Gibeon when Saul appeared before him, and was by him anointed as future king of Israel.†

As we had many places to visit that day, we did not linger upon the windy tower any longer than was needful to take in the wide prospect, and then we went in search of the horses in order to depart to Gibeon. We found these patient animals in charge of the victors, who were holding them by the bridle reins; but those who had been worsted in the fight were determined to have their share of the backshish, and so they seized upon the stirrups, the manes, and even the tails of the horses. Under such circumstances our departure was somewhat embarrassing; but scattering the little coins behind us we rushed through the throng, and, amid yells and angry gestures, went on toward Gibeon.

A half hour's ride brought us to the peculiar-

---

* *Neby Samwil* was regarded by the Crusaders as the site of ancient Shiloh. In later times it was supposed to be the site of Ramathaim Zophim. Robinson, Porter, and others regard it as the site of Mizpeh, which Conder treats as merely a conjecture.— *Ed. Am. S. S. Union.*

† 1 Samuel 9:19; 10:1.

EL JIB (GIBEON).

shaped hill on which ancient Gibeon was situated, and where the little village *el Jib* now stands as its successor.* In descending the steep side of *Neby Samwil*, we had the rounded summit of Gibeon constantly before us, and could note the horizontal terraces which girt it about on the south, and the pleasant pasture lands which lie along its slopes.

Passing over a part of the great mound we came to the miserable village perched against the hillside, with dwellings built of stone, set down without any regard to order or convenience. The inhabitants were squalid and wretched-looking people, and seemed to rival their neighbors on Mizpeh in their utter disregard of cleanliness, and in their eagerness for the ever-expected backshish. The usual number of dogs made their onset upon us as we approached, and by their loud barking warned the other inhabitants, who

---

* The peasantry say that the ancient site of Gibeon stood on the southern or higher part of this hill. The hill is about 200 feet high, naturally a strong site, well supplied with water and covered with vines and olives. Eight springs issue from the sides of the hill. The most famous of these springs issues in a rock-cut chamber about 30 feet long, 7 feet wide, and 7 feet high. The water is clear and abundant. Close to this spring is a rock-cut chamber finished in rough masonry, which is regarded as sacred, and above the spring cave is a paved platform for prayer. The spring is one of the most sacred and venerated in Palestine.—*Ed. Am. S. S. Union.*

came to the doorways to gaze at us, and demand a present. Just below the village we found a fine spring of water, which issues from a rocky cavern and collects in a large pond near by. Not far from this point, we rode over a fallen stone fence into an olive orchard, where our guide hastened to prepare the luncheon, while the other attendants brought water from the spring.

Ancient towns were commonly located upon a hill near a spring or other water supply, so as to secure the inhabitants against enemies, and furnish them with water in case of a siege. Gibeon furnishes both these requirements, and consequently was the site of a Canaanitish town before the conquest under Joshua. The fear of this great conqueror, whose victories at Jericho and Ai had been told throughout the land, led the Gibeonites to adopt the expedient of wearing old clothes and carrying mouldy bread when they appeared before him, in order that they might deceive him with the pretext that they were from a "far country," and so make a league with him.*
Their penalty, to be "hewers of wood and drawers of water," they could readily fulfill, for both wood and water must always have been abundant in Gibeon. The place will ever be famous also in connection with Joshua's battle with "the five

* Joshua 9.

kings," when he commanded the sun to stand still upon Gibeon and the moon in the valley of Ajalon.*

Gibeon was the scene of the magnificent ceremonial with which Solomon inaugurated his reign, when he offered the thousand burnt offerings here.† The sacrifice of a thousand victims was an act of royal magnificence suited to the greatness of Solomon, and scarcely outdone by Xerxes, who offered a thousand oxen at Troy, as Herodotus relates. Here also Solomon had his famous dream, and offered his model prayer that he might have wisdom as a ruler. We found a mound of burnt clay on the top of Gibeon, it may be at Solomon's altar, unless indeed he sacrificed upon *Neby Samwil*.

Upon our return from a ramble over Gibeon we set out again for Jerusalem. Our route now lay to the eastward, along the old road which came up from the plain of Sharon by Wady Suleiman, and intersected the Damascus road near " Gibeah of Saul." As usual we found only a bridle path, instead of a highway, where our horses had to select a safe place for their feet among the loose stones which had fallen in the track.

We only paused to note the location of " Gibeah of Saul " in passing, and to notice the site of an-

---

* Joshua 10 : 12.   † 1 Kings 3 : 4.

cient Nob, which is situated at the foot of Gibeah, as *el Jib* is related to *Neby Samwil*. As we passed Nob the tragic scene in the life of David, when as a fugitive from the court of Saul he came here, and in his extremity of hunger ate of the "shew bread" with his men, came up afresh to our minds.*

We were now on the great Damascus road and proceeding southward toward Jerusalem. Ancient Anathoth lay on the height of ground to the eastward, and was in plain sight from the ridge of Scopus, which we had now reached again. Here and there fields of growing wheat were seen, and at intervals orchards of olive and almond trees grew by the wayside.

When we were about half a mile from the city we dismounted to view the tombs of the Kings.† Like the tombs of the Judges they were

---

* 1 Samuel 21 : 6.

† The so-called *tombs of the Kings* are known to the natives as *Kabur es Salatan* or "tombs of the Sultan." Modern Jews call them the *tomb of Kalba Shebuya*, a mythical rich man. Robinson identified them as the *tomb of Helena*. Three pyramids were visible east of the north road in the fourth century, and noticed by Eusebius. The rolling stone at the door described by Pausanias in the second century is still there. De Saulcy found a sarcophagus in this tomb with an Aramaic inscription roughly cut and approaching square Hebrew in form. He read in the first line "Queen Sara," which it has been conjectured was the native name of Queen Helena, and the body found

originally excavated in the face of a cliff, but in this instance the earth and stone apparently had been removed, in order to expose the face of the rock sufficiently for the purpose designed.

That these tombs were as elaborate as they were extensive, and were fitted up in royal style, is evident from the remains of fine sculpture still traceable upon the face of the cliff. Over the centre of the portal are carved large clusters of grapes between garlands of flowers, intermingled with Corinthian capitals and other decorations, below which is tracery-work of flowers and fruits extending quite across the portal and hanging down along the sides. This is said to be the finest specimen of sculpture existing in or around Jerusalem.

With lamps in hand, furnished by our provident guide, we stooped down and entered the low doorway, and found ourselves in an ante-chamber 18½ by 19 feet in its dimensions. At the south side of this chamber we found the entrances to two other rooms, which we explored successively and noted the crypts arranged along their sides. These rooms were about 12 feet square, and in

along with the sarcophagus may also have been her own. A number of Roman coins were also found, all earlier than the time of Titus, and a sculptured head of Hadrian was found near the tombs.—*Ed. Am. S. S. Union.*

every part gave evidence of their originally elegant construction. We next entered a third room, nearly 13 feet square, finer than any that we had seen, having three crypts on each of three sides. Beyond this was a fourth room, in size nearly equal to the others, with like receptacles for the dead. Fragments of marble lay about, indicating the fact that the interior had been originally lined with this costly material. Over each crypt was a small triangular excavation, in which a lamp could be conveniently placed during the process of entombment.

As to the antiquity of these tombs we have no certain data. Tradition affirms that they were constructed for the kings of Judah, but Josephus intimates that they were built by Helena of Adiabene in connection with the family of the Herods. In either case they have come down from a remote antiquity, and, as their appearance indicates, were intended as the resting-places for the members of a royal household.

As we emerged into the light of day our attention was directed to the apparatus used in closing the cavern. This was a most curiously-fitted stone door, which could only be opened by means of a lever moving it along a grooved passage, and was secured in its place by another slab, also set in a groove, placed at right angles to the door;

the whole arrangement was carefully concealed by a huge flagstone. The stone door was in size and shape not unlike a large grindstone, with the orifice for the lever in the centre, and the groove so prepared that this stone could be rolled along

ROLLING STONE BEFORE TOMB.

it upon its circumference. We were forcibly reminded of the question of the devoted women who came early to the tomb of Jesus, and said, "Who shall roll us away the stone from the door of the sepulchre? And when they looked, they saw that the stone was rolled away: for it was very great."* Was not the tomb of the rich man, Joseph, furnished with this kind of a groove with a circular stone to fit it, thus to be rolled in front of the entrance and sealed when the tomb was to be closed, and to be rolled away again when the sepulchre was to be opened?

While meditating upon this matter we resumed

* Mark 16 : 3, 4.

the saddle and rode forward to Jeremiah's Grotto, which lies only a few hundred yards from the Damascus Gate. It is a huge natural cavern, nearly round, some forty paces in diameter, and perhaps thirty feet high in the middle. The roof of this cavern was anciently connected with the hill named Bezetha, now within the city walls, and its wide, yawning front has been formed by the cutting of a wide avenue between it and the north wall of the city. Some locate the site of Calvary near this grotto. An old Mohammedan has charge of this curiosity, and has his dwelling and a garden in front of the cavern, with a fence surrounding it; this arrangement enables him to collect an extortionate fee for entrance.

Close by this place, and at a point near the Damascus Gate, we were admitted by a low doorway, almost concealed by a bank of earth, into a much larger cavern known as Solomon's Quarries. The low, square door is directly under the city wall, and is only opened by the initiated for the gratification of persevering tourists. After we had passed through the door we were compelled to crawl upon hands and knees for quite a distance, when we found ourselves on the edge of a vast incline dipping under the hill Bezetha. Our lamps having been lighted we stood upright, and by their flickering light began to peer out into the vast abyss before us. Our guide led the way down the slope, and we followed full of wonder. We were in an immense cave, not unlike Jeremiah's Grotto in appearance but vastly larger in dimensions. We went on and on, apparently in a southeasterly direction, our lights failing to reveal either side of the cavern to our sight, and scarcely sufficing to indicate the great altitude of the ceiling. At last we came to a kind of dripping spring, beyond which our guide positively refused to advance, protesting that he would not be responsible for any injury which might befall us if we persisted in our attempt to reach the limits of these vast excavations. Leaving him to listen to the gloomy "drip, drip" of the falling water, we proceeded, penetrating into lower and yet lower levels, until we came to an abrupt ascent, along the rugged edges of which we clambered, peering into the crevices until satisfied that we had now arrived at the southern extremity of this truly wonderful place. The quarry marks were more abundant here, the yellow, chalky limestone having been worked out in rough blocks, some of which had never been removed from the quarry.

Above us, we knew, were the houses and streets of the city, but we had no means of locating our position on the surface; yet we felt sure that we were near the *Via Dolorosa*. Is it not probable that the materials for the ancient temple were actually quarried here from the roof and sides of a natural cavern, and raised by a shaft to the surface of the temple enclosure? We made our way back again to our guide, who seemed to rejoice that we had escaped unharmed, and gaining the entrance once more we returned to our lodgings weary with the fatiguing labors of the day, but gratified nevertheless with all its experiences.

A few moments of leisure enabled us to visit the Jaffa Gate to inspect the "Needle's Eye," which we found to be a small door hung upon hinges in one of the great gates, to admit foot passengers after the hour of closing. It would be difficult indeed for a camel to pass through this aperture, though not impossible. The Scripture reference was well elucidated by the actual sight.*

Needle's Eye.

* Matthew 19 : 24.

CHAPTER X.

TOUR TO THE DEAD SEA AND THE JORDAN.

The time had now arrived when we were to leave Jerusalem, for the long tour northward, by the way of the Dead Sea and the Jordan. Gladly would we have remained longer to verify our first impressions of all the interesting places in and around the holy city; but the guides had the preparations completed and the itinerary arranged.

On the morning of Tuesday, April 8, we were early astir, and eagerly observing the incidents of street life, and the locations of greatest interest, that we might retain a more vivid recollection of all the places we had already visited. While standing thus expectant on the balcony of the hotel overlooking David's Street, we were gratified with the sight of a primitive procession, composed of country people, on their way to the Mosque of Omar. The company was composed of about fifty persons, all poorly clad, but with some gaudy-colored sashes and turbans sprinkled among them, with the intent of presenting a festive or military appearance. They had several dingy banners in sight, and all made a ludicrous attempt at keeping step on the rough, slippery pavement to the music of the cymbal and tom-tom.

We were interested most of all in the figure of a young man, who led the straggling procession and performed the office of dancer as well as he was able on such precarious footing. He was a strange-looking youth, perhaps twenty years of age, of tall and spare figure, with long yellow hair streaming out from under his high turban, and a wild, wandering look in his eyes. His countenance was grave, and his shuffling step, emphasized from time to time by the stroke of his tall spear-handle upon the pavement, indicated that he was engaged in a religious solemnity. We were at once reminded of the dancing of King David when he brought the ark to Zion. Not unlike this young man must he have appeared when, girded with a linen ephod, he danced before the Lord with all his might, and, in reply to the taunt of the proud Michal, said, "*It was* before the Lord, which chose me . . . ruler . . . over Israel; therefore will I play before the Lord. And I will yet be more vile than thus, and will be base in mine own sight."* How little change, we thought, has three thousand years wrought in the customs of this city of the great king!

* 2 Samuel 6 : 14–22.

Many final tasks had to be performed upon our departure from Jerusalem. Trinkets of olive wood, photographs, and a few necessaries of clothing had to be laid in. We went to bid adieu to our obliging consul, Colonel Wilson, and deposit with him our letters for home. Then we repaired to the group of horses drawn up near the tower of David, and made choice of the animals we were to ride, each one fully convinced that he had been allotted the most undesirable steed—a conviction which was daily strengthened as we advanced on our journey. The sun was well up over the Mount of Olives when our party, now enlarged by the addition of three English clergymen and two Americans, swept past the Damascus Gate, crossed the Kedron once more, and fell into the main road to Jericho. At the angle in the road where Jesus beheld the city and wept over it we paused again, to take our parting view, and bid farewell to the earthly Jerusalem. We were soon beyond Bethany, going down the steep cliffs toward Jordan. Our route now lay over precipices, along the sides of which rough paths have been worn by the feet of passing animals. The face of these seamed and furrowed masses of dry, yellow-colored limestone is desolate enough surely to satisfy the Abyssinian monks who have haunted these caves for ages past.

The whole forenoon was occupied in scrambling down from one terrace and cliff to another. The sun smote the yellow surface with a blinding glare, and we were glad to secure the shade of turbans and umbrellas, while we held on to the saddle-pommels with a firm grip as our horses picked their way through the ragged notches of the rocks.

The ruins of an old khan nearly midway in the descent are supposed to mark the site of the parable of the good Samaritan. Even to this day one going down from Jerusalem to Jericho may fall among thieves. There is no law or order, we are told, in this part of Palestine, no protection to citizens or travellers except what they provide for themselves. The natives around the coasts of the Dead Sea consist of small tribes, generally at war with each other and waiting for convenient opportunities for plunder.

Our guides had taken pains to secure us a safe escort in the persons of two sheikhs, who make a business of conducting tourists through their territory upon the payment of large backshish. They were warlike men, of swarthy skin, savage glance and sinister expression. Of course they were our friends now, on account of the dear backshish, and they were even our intimate brothers. They would ride familiarly by our side, turn the bilious pupils of their wary eyes upon us, and playfully handle the pistols, swords, dirks, lances, long guns, etc., etc., with which they were decorated.

The sheikhs were mounted upon splendid horses, trained to the saddle and obedient to the riders' very nod. One of them was a fiery, coal-black steed, with heavy, flowing mane and tail, his bridle decorated with scarlet tassels at the ears, and long leather fringe across the front and at the throat-latch. The saddle was low in the pommel, with strong girth and back-strap and long pendants streaming from the saddle-cloth on either side. Thus equipped and accoutred, the sheikhs would occasionally deploy from us, and ride proudly on in advance as if in quest of foe-men worthy of their steel.

Well toward midday we were startled at the sight of an armed Arab horseman, coming over the crest of a hill at full gallop, with his long lance set as if prepared for a hostile engagement. Our sheikh put the spurs to his black charger, and dashed off to meet the stranger. The two riders continued their course straight as an arrow, with unslackened speed until within a few yards of meeting, when one of them put up his hand by way of salute, and both instantly reined in their steeds in a way that nearly threw them back upon their haunches. Then followed hand-shakings and other demonstrations of friendship as their horses walked quietly onward side by side, as if to accommodate their riders during conversation. Presently the stranger set spurs to his steed, and disappeared down the slope of the Wady Kelt.*

We were now approaching a cluster of low buildings plastered over with mud, named by the Mohammedans *Neby Mûsa*, that is, the tomb of Moses.† Though the Bible declares that Moses died in the land of Moab, and was mysteriously buried in a valley there, and no man knoweth of his sepulchre unto this day, yet the followers of

---

* " The Wady Kelt is a deep narrow gorge, flanked by precipitous cliffs, above which rise white chalk hills, presenting a tangled network of narrow water-worn torrent beds, with knife-edged ridges between. The slopes are very steep, and numerous conical peaks and rounded knolls project along the ridges." Where the wady crosses the plain of the Jordan, it becomes a broad water-course covered with water-worn boulders and shingle, running between banks 20 to 30 feet high and 150 to 300 feet apart. The Wady Kelt has been suggested as identical with the brook Cherith, where Elijah was fed by ravens. See *Survey of Palestine*, vol. iii. p. 168.—*Ed. Am. S. S. Union.*

† *Neby Mûsa* is a deserted mosque, with a short minaret. There is a cenotaph shown in the mosque as the tomb of Moses. The place was built 668 A.H., and the minaret in 880 A.H.=1502 A.D. The spot is visited yearly in April by a great crowd of Mohammedan pilgrims, accompanied by half-naked fanatical dervishes, who parade the streets of Jerusalem all the previous morning shouting, " *La ilaha ill Allah!*"—*Ed. Am. S. S. Union.*

the false prophet have located his grave here on the west side of the Jordan.* We had seen many of the pilgrims on their way to the festival now in progress here, both on the road from Hebron and also in coming down from Bethany. Many of the men were on foot, but the women and children were seated in panniers on the backs of donkeys.

Our route lay a little southward of this place, now filled with the stir and bustle of constantly-arriving pilgrims, and on the height of ground just beyond we dismounted for luncheon. We were now on the lowest of the mountain terraces overlooking the Dead Sea. The surroundings were dismal in the extreme. Not a tree, shrub, or scarcely a blade of grass enlivened the prospect. Under the fierce rays of the sun, we sat down upon the raw earth around the rug and cloth where the attendants had laid out the bread, cold meats, eggs and oranges. On the flat roof of the one-story mosque opposite, a long line of men were performing their devotions, with their faces turned toward Mecca. They went through their bowings, kneelings and prostrations with a regularity and monotony that was painful to witness. Just then the sound of the tom-tom was heard, a gun was fired, and a great procession

* Deuteronomy 34 : 6.

of pilgrims, with banners flying, marched into the place, and were received with much ado by those who had arrived before them. The whole scene was in keeping with the barren environs. The strange customs of nations were represented there as well as the blight of nature.

Within an hour of the time of our arrival we were again in the saddle, hastening on towards the blue expanse of waters spread out at our feet, which at this distance did not appear at all like a sea of death, but rather like a beautiful lake in some northern state in America. Upon reaching the plain of the Jordan we passed through a strip of dry jungle, and emerged upon a shelving beach, composed of salt, sand, and some sort of alkali, where there was not a sign of indigenous vegetation. Wrecks of trees lay strewn upon the surface, encrusted in salt, their ragged broken limbs presenting an appearance like the valley of dry bones in Ezekiel's vision. The heat was not as intense here as we had anticipated. A breeze from the southeast had sprung up, and brought with it the welcome shadow of a passing cloud, and thus relieved the usual pressure of the atmosphere. Without delay we prepared for a bath, anxious to test the old theory that nothing can sink beneath these waters. Mr. H., to whom the reader has been

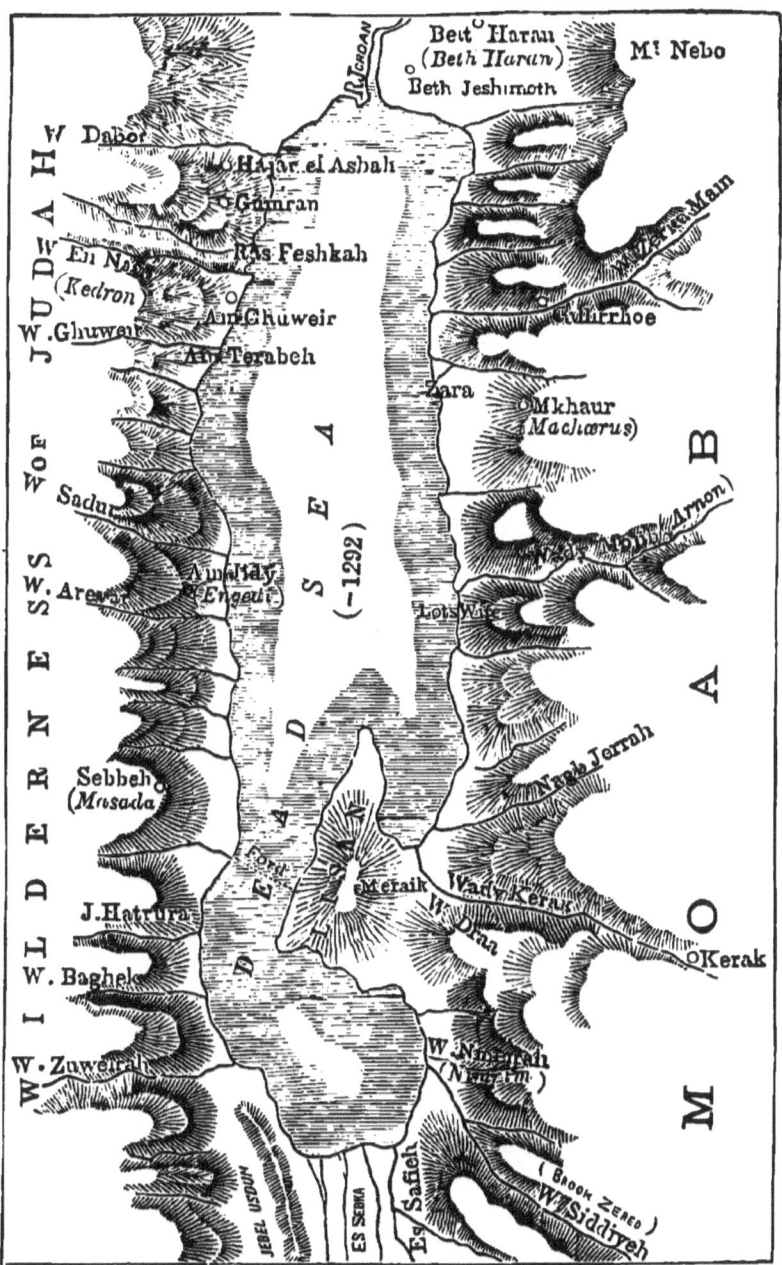

THE SALT OR DEAD SEA. (*After Sketch by Major Wilson.*)

introduced at Ramleh, declared his doubts of all these declarations of the ancients, and was the first to plunge into the waters to confirm his stout denial. He obtained more than he had bargained for, inasmuch as he pushed out a little too far from shore, and the heavy surf raised by the wind quickly submerged him. He came back to terra firma gasping and weeping, and certainly the tears he shed that day were very salt and bitter. The rest of the party fared but little better. The specific gravity and levitating power of the water were evidently very great, but, on account of the heavy waves which beat upon the body like sheets of lead, we could get no fair opportunity to test it. Added to this was the discomfort experienced in breathing. The water was so salt, bitter and pungent that it affected the nostrils to such a degree as almost to produce strangulation, while the smarting of the eyes and each little abrasion of the skin produced not only discomfort, but positive suffering. Notwithstanding all, we tried the experiment of floating, and found that head and feet could scarcely be submerged, the heavy part of the body alone settling under the surface, yet not sufficiently to necessitate the action of the limbs to prevent sinking. In the use of the towel after the bath we found the body covered with a pitchy substance, which left an unpleasant sensation for us after dressing.

After this novel experience we mounted again, and hastened across the plain toward the Jordan. The surface was generally level, with here and there a shallow wady, and the whole was without vegetation. The deep sand deposit was mingled with salt, gypsum, sulphur and other ingredients, and hindered the progress of our already wearied horses. At four o'clock we came upon the steep terrace which borders the rushing river at the usual ford and bathing-place of the pilgrims. Here we dismounted and proceeded to bathe, as all dutiful pilgrims have done for ages immemorial, and were the more eager to do so in order to wash away the unpleasant traces of our late bath in the Dead Sea. We found the water shallow near the shore, but the "shingle" was so sharp that we could hardly stand up against the rushing flood. The fall of the Jordan, as is well known, is very great; hence its name, "The Descender," and hence the mystery of the miracle by which the Israelites crossed it when swollen by the spring freshets.

The water was of a yellow, muddy color, not, like the Dead Sea, of a beautiful blue; but it was sweet and pure, and thus a fitting emblem of the sacrament of Christian baptism. Upon

PILGRIMS' BATHING-PLACE.—THE RIVER JORDAN.

regaining the shore and our garments we loitered upon the upper bank among the tamarisk, agnus castus, white poplar and other trees, mingled with which was a heavy growth of cane and reeds. Of the latter I cut three fine specimens,

REEDS. (*Schaff's "Popular Commentary."*)

one of which still remains in my collection, a cherished memorial. It is about twelve feet in length, with but little taper, graceful and pliant, moved by each breath of air, with a soft feathery plume at the top one foot in length. It is, without doubt, the "reed shaken by the wind" to which the Saviour alluded when discoursing of John the Baptist.*

In these waters, perhaps at this very spot, our Lord was baptized of John, thus, as he said, "fulfilling all righteousness." Crowds of anx-

* Matthew 11 : 7.

ious souls then thronged these banks, coveting the application of the cleansing water, as a token that their sins were forgiven. And in after ages what multitudes have come hither to bathe in these sacred waters and tarry upon these shaded banks, where even now the bulbul and the thrush in their sweet song answer back to the murmur and ceaseless chatter of the restless current rippling over its shingly bed.

The breadth of the river is not great, now, at its ordinary height, not above four or five rods in width; but earlier in the season, when the "swellings" take place, and Jordan is in his strength, what a mighty flood then pours down this deep gorge to the sea of death! Thus it doubtless was when the Israelites first crossed it, under Joshua, to enter the "promised land." But Jehovah, who brought them hither from Egypt, made a way for them to pass over in safety, as he will make a way for his saints to pass over the Jordan of death safe into the true land of promise, where he will give his people rest in "the land that is very far off." Watts and Stennett have associated this river with thoughts of solemn import in their imperishable verses, in which they draw a beautiful parallel between the Israelites, waiting on yonder shore, and the dying Christian.

> "On Jordan's stormy banks I stand,
>   And cast a wishful eye
> To Canaan's fair and happy land,
>   Where my possessions lie.
>
> "Sweet fields beyond the swelling flood
>   Stand dressed in living green ;
> So to the Jews old Canaan stood,
>   While Jordan rolled between."

Pleasant as it was to linger at the ford, we were presently warned by our guide that it was time for us to resume our journey toward the camp. Our course now lay almost due westward across the plain, here some six miles in width. We were now on the track of the ancient Israelites as they marched toward Gilgal and Jericho. At the farther side of the plain, and directly confronting us, stood the great landmark of the whole region, named Mount Quarantania. This massive wall of rock, which lifts its majestic front twelve hundred feet in the air, with its sides gilded by the rays of the declining sun, presented a truly grand appearance. Its name indicates that it was the scene of the Saviour's trial when, for forty days, he fasted in the wilderness and endured the temptation. When we had crossed about two-thirds of the distance from the river to the mountain we came to a poor hamlet named *Eriha*. The miserable dwellings of the *Ghawarineh* tribe, to which our valiant sheikhs belonged, are here grouped around an ancient castle, below which were a few unfenced plots of cultivated ground and some enclosures of fruit trees. This spot is supposed to mark ancient Gilgal,* the first place consecrated to religious worship by the Israelites after entering the promised land.† This tribe does not bear a very good reputation, and the inhabitants whom we saw were not at all prepossessing in appearance, and we did not tarry long in their territory.

From this point onward we followed the course of the wady Kelt, whose stream-bed was now

---

* Jericho has occupied more than one, and perhaps three different sites at different periods of its history. Old Jericho of Joshua's time was destroyed. Its site is generally placed at *Tell es Sultan*, near '*Ain es Sultan*, or the spring of the Sultan, popularly called "Elisha's Fountain." This is about one and a half miles northwest of the modern hamlet *Eriha*. The Jericho of the New Testament period, and which Christ visited, is identified by the *Palestine Survey* with *el Aleik*, about one and a half miles west of *Eriha*, and the same distance west of south of "Elisha's Fountain." The Jericho of the crusading period is identified with *Eriha*, a miserable mud hamlet surrounded by a thorny briar (*Zizyphus spina Christi*, the Christ-thorn). Gilgal of the Jordan valley was located by Thomson and others near the modern hamlet *Eriha*, but the *Palestine Survey*, with apparently greater precision, identifies it with a mound or ruin one and a half miles east of *Eriha*, and called *Jiljulieh*. It is on the direct road from *Hajlah* to '*Ain es Sultan*, and about four and a half miles from the Jordan.—*Ed. Am. S. S. Union.*

† Joshua 5: 10.

INHABITANTS AND DWELLINGS AT ERIHA (JERICHO OF THE CRUSADES).

filled with clear running water, along the margin of which we found a luxuriant growth of nûbk trees and wild shrubbery. From the branches of one of these shrubs we obtained a number of specimens of the apples of Sodom, which, according to the legend, are fair as to outward appearance, but within are full of ashes. The fruit, if such it may be called, is not unlike a wild plum in appearance. It has a bright yellow skin, attractive to the eye indeed, but when broken open not even a seed or a grain of ashes is visible. It is an apt symbol of the utter emptiness of mere outward pretension.

Turning northward from the Kelt, we soon came to the bank of another purling stream, and at its source found our tents pitched, beside *'Ain es Sultan*, or Elisha's Fountain, and the attendants waiting to receive us. We were now under the foot of Mount Quarantania, and the shadows of its mighty presence warned us of approaching darkness. After we had partaken of our evening meal we sat in the tent door, listening to the cheerful croaking of the frogs at the fountain, and looking for the familiar stars as they came out one by one with their welcome light to cheer us. The adventures of the day were rehearsed with zest, the mules and horses meanwhile munching the barley and beans from their nose-bags, while the sound of the gurgling waters near by invited to slumber. A little later, as we were reclining upon our couches within the tent, preparatory to retiring for the night, one of our company suddenly started up, with the exclamation that he saw the figure of a man crouched in the doorway as if about to effect a stealthy entrance. Soon after a gun was discharged in the camp, which, we found upon inquiry, was simply a device of our guide to warn the natives that we were on the alert for any prowlers who might wish to secure plunder. The sheikhs were to remain on watch all night around the camp-fire, as an additional warrant of security that our slumbers might not be disturbed by fears of a midnight adventure. But the stamping of the horses, the ringing of the bells on the necks of the sumpter-mules, and the howling of the jackals on Quarantania left us little time for sound sleeping.

CHAPTER XI.

FROM JERICHO TO THE VALLEY OF BACA.

Our first night in camp at '*Ain es Sultan,* while not particularly restful to us after the most fatiguing day of our journey to the Dead Sea and

'AIN ES SULTAN, OR FOUNTAIN OF ELISHA. (*After Photographs.*)

the Jordan, was nevertheless a valuable experience. The situation of the camp was altogether favorable to lovers of the beautiful in nature, and of the free life in tent and saddle. With these surroundings even the most staid townsman would be tempted to extol the life of the wandering gypsies. At this place Canon Tristram spent many days in camp in 1864, while making his

(183)

valuable observations in ornithology and geology, and investigating the physical features of the plain of the Jordan. His descriptions give us the idea that he had something like a hunter's camp here at 'Ain es Sultan, and that the poor chats, sun-birds, doves and swallows suffered more from the discharge of firearms than did the wolves and jackals of the mountains, or the leopards and wild boars, which had been driven from their lairs by the winter freshets of the Jordan.

However this may have been, the camping-ground at 'Ain es Sultan is truly a delightful place. The natural features of mountains for protection from bleak winds, vegetation and fresh flowing water for refreshment, and the wide, fertile plain, the river beyond, the sea below and the distant wall of Moab in the background for scenery, altogether make up a delightful landscape.

Just as the gray light of morning began to spread over the distant fields of Moab I arose, and, hastily making my toilet, with field-glass and note-book in hand sallied forth to make observations. Hard by the tents I came upon the fountain which is the source of life and fertility to such a large district of the plain below. To dash the hands and face into the sweet and copious current was indeed refreshing. This is supposed to be the fountain which Elisha purified with salt, the waters of which were thereby healed that there should not be from thence any more death or barren land.* From the fact that the inhabitants of Jericho said to Elisha, "The situation of this city is pleasant, but the water is naught" (*i. e.*, "bad" or brackish), in response to which he performed the miracle, it appears that the city was situated near by the fountain, or on the stream below it. The spring would also naturally be within the enclosure of the walled town which Joshua overthrew, for the inhabitants would not be apt to leave the source of water supply without the walls, where the besiegers might easily cut it off. Besides *'Ain es Sultan* is so situated that Joshua might have marched round its adjacent city, just as the narrative of the Bible describes, for the foot of Quarantania is nearly half a mile distant toward the west.

Upon leaving the fountain I climbed to the top of a large mound or hummock only a few rods distant, under which may lie the ruins of ancient Jericho. From this point a wide prospect was opened to view. *Eriha*, with its ancient tower, appeared to stand in a line with the north end of the Dead Sea, about one-third of the way distant. The only traces of the Jordan visible

* 2 Kings 2 : 21.

were the trees on its banks, beyond which in plain sight lay the uplands of Perea or Gilead. The waters of the Dead Sea were also in sight, and a kind of purple mist hung over its eastern side, under the long, high wall or cliff of Moab. The notch at the mouth of the Zerka Main wady, in which the hot springs of Callirrhóe are situated, was plainly visible. The waters of the sea were sky blue in color, and appeared to be entirely tranquil, as there was no breeze. What a mystery surrounds this wonderful sheet of water! "Reposing in its deep chasm or caldron, without any current or outlet, its heavy waters impregnated with mineral salts, combined with asphaltum and sulphur, acrid and nauseous to the taste, and fatal to animal and vegetable life; no fin stirring in its still depths, and no flowers or foliage fringing its borders; its shores and surrounding territory sterile, desolate and dreary; the whole region lonely and stern, and bearing marks of some dread convulsion of nature; the cemetery of cities that once occupied a portion of its site, and a perpetual memorial of the righteous judgments of God."* The whole western shore, though without forest land, is described in the New Testament as the wilderness of Judea. Here and there, where fresh-water streams empty

* Smith's Bible Dictionary.

into the sea, shrubbery and vegetation appear, as at '*Ain Feshkha*, but generally the aspect is utterly desolate. Its surface is twelve hundred and ninety-two feet below the Mediterranean or ocean level, and its deepest bottom is about thirteen hundred feet below its surface. It is forty miles in length, and from nine to ten miles in width, and no open chasm of equal depression is known to exist elsewhere on the globe. All its waters are carried off by evaporation under the sun's rays, which at this extraordinary depth exert an influence like an immense fire on the surface of a great caldron.*

* The depression of the Dead Sea below the level of the Mediterranean Sea varies from 2 to 3 feet, being greater at some periods of the year than at others; and Robinson holds that it has varied from 10 to 15 feet within the last fifty years. Russegger in 1838 by barometer computed the depression to be about 1400 feet; Symonds in 1840 by trigonometrical survey made it 1312 feet; Dale of Lynch's Expedition in 1848 calculated that it was 1316 feet; more careful measurements by Duc de Luynes and Lieut. Vignes of the French navy in 1864 made it 1286 feet; and a still more scientific survey by English engineers under Capt. Wilson in March, 1865, found it to be 1292 feet, but computed that it was $2\frac{1}{2}$ feet higher owing to winter freshets than at other periods of the year, hence the least depression would be $1289\frac{1}{2}$ feet. The greatest depth of the Dead Sea is in the northern portion, which Lieut. Symonds (1841) measured at 1350 feet; but Lieut. Dale of Lynch's Expedition (1848) found it to be 1308 feet, and a later measurement agrees very nearly, making it 1310 feet. Its *mean* depth according to Lynch is 1080 feet.—*Ed. Am. S. S. Union.*

The location of the cities of the plain, Sodom and Gomorrah, is still an unsettled question. Some authorities favor the hypothesis that the

THE DEAD SEA FROM JEBEL USDUM (MOUNTAIN OF SALT): SOUTH END.
(*After Tristram.*)

cities of the plain were at the north end of the Dead Sea, and not far from Jericho. But Dr. Robinson inclines to the more ancient theory that they were located at the south end of the sea, and that "the plain" is now in part occupied by the southern bay, below the peninsula *el Lisan*.*
Canon Tristram, when at Wady Mahawat at the southwest corner of the sea, found large masses of bitumen mingled with gravel, overlying a thin

* *Researches*, vol. ii. p. 604.

stratum of sand, so strongly impregnated with sulphur that it yielded powerful fumes on being sprinkled over a hot coal. He says, "If there be any physical evidence left of the catastrophe which destroyed Sodom and Gomorrah we have it here. The whole appearance points to a shower of hot sulphur and an irruption of bitumen upon it, which would naturally be calcined and impregnated by fumes." And yet the Canon seems afterward to favor the northern hypothesis.*

While I was sitting upon the mound at 'Ain es Sultan the sun sprang up over Moab, and flooded the summit of Mount Quarantania with his golden light, and the cooing of doves and the matins of the spring birds about its foot drew my attention to its majestic surface. Far up its front I could see the caverns where the monks long ago lived and died in the practice of their strict asceticism. Some of these caverns are said to be

---

* In his later work, *The Land of Moab*, he writes: "It seems evident, on a careful examination of the scriptural account of 'the cities of the plain,' that they must have been situated in the 'ciccar' or 'ghor' of Jordan, at the north end of the Dead Sea. There is no reason, from the details given us in Scripture, for assigning to the cities of the plain a location on the west, rather than the east, side of that river; and as the plain of Shittim is much more extensive than that of Jericho, and the Jordan possesses three fords, passable, except during the season of the floods, in its lower reach, it is probable that some, at least, of the four cities were on the farther side." Pages 331–334.

formed into chapels, with chambers above them where the anchorets of the fourth century lived, and back of which their tombs are now to be seen, having their bones, covered with dust, within them. On the very summit of the mountain the remains of a ruined chapel were plainly visible, and on either side of it were the wadys Kelt and 'Ain Duk, the former a deep gulch, in the recesses of which is the traditional spot where Elijah was fed by the ravens.

SYCAMORE.

On the banks of the stream which issues from this gorge and flows past *Eriha*, but at a higher point, *el Aleik*, it is supposed the Jericho built by Herod the Great was situated. Graphic descriptions remain of the baths, the circus, the groves of palm and fruit trees which then covered this whole region. The palms have long since disappeared, because uncultivated or unprotected; but the warmth of temperature here is like that of Egypt, and the palms and all tropical fruits might again flourish with proper cultivation. Our Saviour passed through Jericho when he healed the blind men, and when he called Zaccheus down from the branches of the sycamore. One or two specimens of this tree, the fig sycamore, still remain in the jungle at the mouth of the gorge, as if to attest the certainty of the location.*

After an early breakfast the tents were struck, and we were once more in the saddle pursuing our way along the brook formed by *'Ain Duk*, whose banks were fringed with a luxuriant growth of cane and shrubbery. While thus riding forward in Indian file along the crooked trail, the sound of music in the distance fell upon our ears. After many vain conjectures as to its origin, we at last caught sight of a group of five or six native girls approaching who were marching to a

---

* As before noted in chapter x., *Eriha* is the accepted site of the Jericho of the crusading era, while *el Aleik* is the proposed site of the Roman or New Testament Jericho. It is one and a half miles above *Eriha*. The Crusaders built a third Jericho at *Eriha* after the Roman Jericho of Christ's time had fallen into decay.—*Ed. Am. S. S. Union.*

tune they were singing, if tune it might be called where the whole performance seemed so much like screeching. For the benefit of all readers of a musical turn of mind the score of their song is here presented :*

As we proceeded up the valley of *'Ain Duk* we were reminded that we were now on the line of march of Joshua with the host of Israel when he ascended to Ai and Bethel, and accomplished his celebrated victory over their inhabitants.† Following the course of the stream through the wide fertile valley, where vegetation and wild fruit

---

* Canon Tristram, when in camp at *'Ain es Sultan*, had a visit from the women of *Eriha*, which he describes as follows: "They came up and formed in front of the tents with loud shouts and the strange 'trill, trill' with the tongue which we had often heard from the women of Algiers. . . . They were a miserable and degraded-looking set, scantily clad in blue cotton, all very filthy, and, excepting two or three of the younger ones, most repulsive in feature. I never saw such vacant, sensual and debased features in any group of human beings of the type and form of whites. There was no trace of mind in the expression of any one of these poor creatures, who scarcely know they have a soul, and have not an idea beyond the day." . . . The evening previous the camp men also gave the Canon a 'fantasia,' with a series of deep guttural grunts in two-four time, accompanied with a clapping of the hands. . . . "An extempore song of endless verses in praise of the Howadjis, confined within three semitones" . . . all for backshish.

† Joshua 8 : 3.

trees appeared on either hand, we came, in the course of two hours, to the foot of the high hills of Ephraim. At this point the valley suddenly became narrow, having steep cliffs on either side. Instead of continuing our route into this gorge, our guide here turned to the south, and commenced to climb the side of the mountain. Here we came upon the traces of an old Roman road, the bed of which had originally been macadamized with excellent slabs of limestone. The road climbed the great elevation by zig-zags, thus reducing the steepness of the grade by increasing the distance to be traversed. While this was a tedious ascent, taxing the energy of both men and horses, we could see from the configuration of the surrounding district that it was the most available route for a wagon-road or thoroughfare between Jerusalem and Jericho. The route by Bethany and the wady Kelt is indeed more direct —only fifteen miles in distance—but on account of the intervening ledges and cliffs it could never have been anything more than a track for footmen or a bridle-path. Hence the construction of this highway, and the zig-zags for ascending to the summit. Doubtless Herod the Great frequently passed over this road in his chariot, with great pomp and circumstance, when on his way to and from his winter palace at Jericho.

When we were midway in the ascent we saw a gazelle bounding away over the height of Quarantania, but were not near enough for our guide to obtain the shot which he coveted. The road now ran westward to the very brink of the gorge, at the bottom of which was a thick jungle. At last, after turning another angle to the eastward, we arrived at the summit, and obtained a grand view of the whole Jordan plain, and of the entire route we had just traversed. The view was similar to that obtained from the mound at 'Ain es Sultan, but much more extensive. The three streams supplied from 'Ain Duk, 'Ain es Sultan and Wady Kelt could be traced by the growth of shrubbery on their banks across the wide plain, with the broader course of the Jordan visible by its fringe of trees at the farther side; while far, far away appeared the hills of Gilead, cleft by the Jabbok, on whose banks Jacob wrestled all night with the mysterious stranger.*

Farther to the south, and across the Dead Sea, we again saw the mountains of Moab, their high cliffs and ragged peaks well revealed in the bright sunlight. It was our last view of the land from which Ruth and Naomi came, when they sought an asylum in their widowhood at Bethlehem.

We now turned westward again, and kept on

* Genesis 32 : 24.

our course over a rough bridle-path not far from the brink of the gorge already described, until we came to a poor hamlet perched upon a hill,

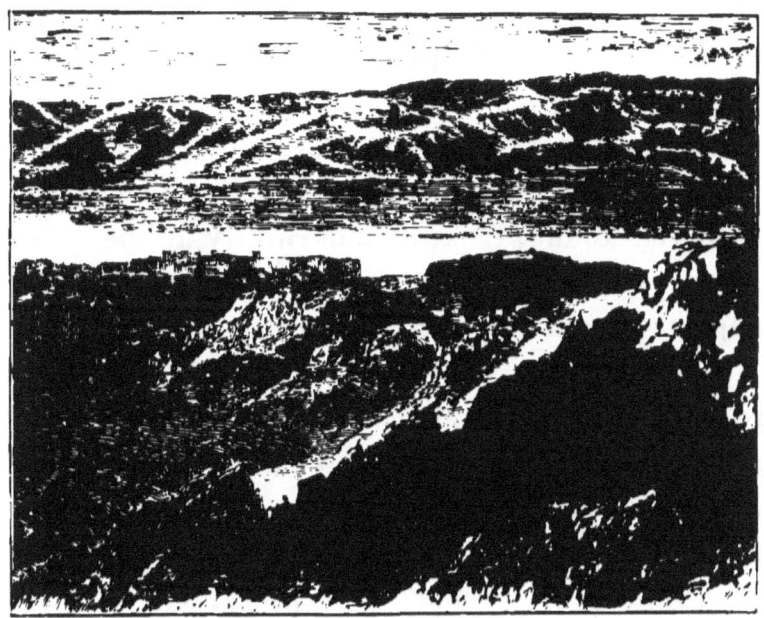

MOUNTAINS OF MOAB.

named *Deir Diwan*. We rode past the place, and halted in an olive orchard near by for luncheon. We had hardly dismounted before we were surrounded by the swarthy, sinister-looking men who inhabit this place. When the guide had prepared the food on the cloth spread upon the ground, and we were seated on its border, *a la Turk*, the hungry-looking men drew nearer still, and patiently watched every mouthful that we ate, hoping, no doubt, that some portion would be assigned to them, but in this they were disappointed. The women did not venture away from their dirty stone dwellings, having been forbidden, no doubt, by these "lords of creation," who coveted the first opportunity to be present at the feast themselves. When the cloth and provision had been removed and we were riding out of the orchard I noticed that the twenty-three men were gathered round, looking mournfully at the place where we had been seated, after which they departed to their village in sadness.

We were now at the head waters of streams running into the Jordan, and in the neighborhood of ancient Bethel. We found here ancient ruins of a town lying on the slopes of two hills facing each other, between which was a reservoir, with heavy walls of masonry well preserved. On the hill to the eastward are the remains of a fortified Christian church, which was probably built by the early Christians to consecrate the spot where Abraham built his second altar after entering the promised land, and where he separated from Lot. The latter, attracted by the apparent fertility of the Jordan valley lying beneath him, contrasted with the barrenness of the stony ravines and ridges on the westward, chose the country of the Jordan, and journeyed eastward to the shores of the Dead Sea. Lieutenant Anderson, whose ideas on the topography of this vicinity are valuable, thinks that the site of Ai may be confidently assigned to a ruined hill-top east of the church near *Deir Diwan*, called by the Arabs *et Tel*, "the heap." This corresponds exactly to the description, when we know the site of Bethel and that of Abraham's encampment, where he built an altar; for we read that he pitched his camp "having Bethel on the west and Hai on the east." There is a valley behind the ruined heap where Joshua placed his ambush. There is also a spot opposite, across the intervening valley, where Joshua stood to give the preconcerted signal; and there is a plain or ridge down which the men of Ai hurried in pursuit of the retreating Israelites, so that the men in ambush rose and captured the city, and made it a heap (or a "tell") forever.[*] In coming up to Bethel from *Deir Diwan* we had the crest of this high ridge on our right hand constantly in sight, from the summit of which Abraham and Lot could look over all the plain of Jordan and the rough ridges of the country afterward assigned to Benjamin and Judah.

At Bethel we came within six miles of the point where we had entered the Damascus road when on our way from Gibeon to Jerusalem. The intervening section of the road is said to follow the

[*] Joshua 8 : 28.

line of the water-shed, and on both sides valleys take their rise, and become at once rocky ravines, descending precipitously on the left hand to the Jordan, and on the right hand more gradually to the Mediterranean. The traveller over these six miles of the land of Benjamin finds nothing but rocks and stones and ruined heaps and low ridges of hills, without a prominent peak or feature to vary the scene; so that we lost but little by not going over this section.

On a slight elevation just to the north of the ruins of Bethel, now named *Beitun,* we found on either side of the highway an immense number of boulders and slabs of stratified rock, well described by Dean Stanley. The track winds through an uneven surface covered, as with gravestones, by large sheets of bare rock, some few here and there standing up like the cromlechs of druidical monuments. Somewhere here, no doubt, Jacob came as an exile from his early home in Beersheba, when he lighted upon a certain place and tarried there all night, because the sun was set; and he took of the stones and put them for his pillows, and lay down in that place to sleep.*
The wanderer's dream of the heavenly ladder may have been suggested by the aspect of the hill to the westward, and on the opposite side of

* Genesis 28 : 11.

a little valley, ribbed, as it is, with parallel layers of rock, which give it the appearance of a majestic stone staircase, like the side of the Pyramid of Cheops, to one resting in a recumbent position. Two of us here fell behind the party, and dismounting from our horses tested the matter by lying down upon the stony surface of the ground, only to find our impressions favorable to the theory. When the rays of the setting sun fell upon that terraced hillside it would appear not unlike a majestic "staircase," which is the more accurate word for the Hebrew "sullam." Whatever may have been the outward cause of the dream, we know that it had an interior meaning which can only be fulfilled in the words, "Hereafter ye shall see heaven open, and the angels of God ascending and descending upon the Son of man."* Jacob had no difficulty here in finding a stone for his pillow; nor was it strange that, when he awoke, he took the stone and consecrated it as a pillar, and said, "How dreadful is this place! this is none other but the house of God (Beth-el), and this is the gate of heaven."†

The lateness of the hour compelled us to hasten forward after the party. We soon came to the head of a narrow glen opening out northward, which we entered by the dry stream bed, having

* John 1 : 51. † Genesis 28 : 16–18.

high stone walls on either side enclosing vineyards. As we advanced, the hills on either side became high and precipitous, the vineyards disappeared, and we found ourselves in the depths of a long, gloomy valley. In the rocky cliffs on either side we noticed a singular conformation, consisting of long tubular galleries occasioned by erosion of water in past geological ages, and which run parallel with the bed of the valley, but at a great height above it.

We continued to wind our way through this singular recess, which has been described as a place of charming melancholy. The valley is narrow and gloomy; a dark water oozes from the rocks, pierced with sepulchres, which form its walls. It may be that this is Baca, or the "valley of tears," or of the "dripping waters," celebrated as one of the stations by the way, when in ancient times the pious pilgrims went up to Jerusalem.* We encamped in that valley for the night at *'Ain el Haramîyeh,* or Robber's Fountain, and slept sweetly after the long ride from the Jordan valley.

* Psalm 84.

CHAPTER XII.

FROM BACA TO THE VALE OF NABLUS.

Our encampment at *'Ain el Haramiyeh*, or Robber's Fountain, was in a picturesque location. On either side of the narrow valley were high hills, fortified by "the munitions of rocks," in the clefts of which we saw the traces of wild honeysuckle and maiden's-hair fern. Far up the heights we heard the partridges clucking to their chickens as the night drew on. On the west side of the glen was a patch of green sward, where our five tents were pitched, and near by the thirty animals, which transported our persons and effects from place to place, were tethered. The brook, with its volume of water largely increased by the spring rains, ran just in front of our location, into which our copious fountain also emptied its constant current.

This location has long been noted as a haunt of robbers, but we were not disturbed by any greater enemy while there than the jackals, which kept up their wild serenade at intervals during the hours of darkness. An old man, travelling with a boy and a forlorn-looking donkey, whom we had passed at Bethel, crept slyly into our camp late in the evening, and, avoiding the notice of the guards, located his sleeping-place against the side of our tent, where his company kept up a continual shuffling and grunting during the night. Our annoyance at this intrusion we quietly endured, however, out of pity for these poor wayfarers, who must have suffered from the cold winds which swept down from the hills, and against which they had only their garments and an old blanket for protection. We could not help thinking that thus, perhaps, Joseph and Mary made their way over this same route, from Nazareth to Bethlehem, just before the first Christmas. The poor people of this land have always travelled in this manner, sleeping in the open air or in the poor khans at night, and with only the meagre contents of their wallets for defence against hunger.

Just as the day began to break the poor man aroused his boy and donkey from their sleep, and hastily departed. Toward evening of the same day we overtook him at Jacob's Well just as he was entering Nablûs. As the Samaritans claim that Mount Gerizim was the mountain where "on the third day Abraham lifted up his eyes and saw the place afar off," we thought of the sorrowful patriarch and his obedient son as we passed the little party, and the language of Genesis reverted at once to our memory—"And Abraham rose up early in the morning, and saddled his ass, and took . . . Isaac his son, . . . and went unto the place of which God had told him."*

The sun was beginning to chase away the shadows from the winding valley and its deep recesses, whose dripping waters are compared to "tears" by the Psalmist, when we set forth upon our day's journey. Scarcely had we crossed the little stream before we met a garrison of Turkish soldiers, on their way from Nablûs to keep the peace during the Easter festivities at Jerusalem. They came on at a quick pace, in broken ranks, and were a hardy-looking band, well used to slim fare, fatigue and exposure. We were, at this point, on the border line between two tribes of Israel. The "vale of weeping" behind us was anciently the pass, or highway, leading down from the heights of Benjamin about Bethel to the pleasant plains of Ephraim, lying farther north. We soon drew near the village of *Sinjil*, and at this place departed from the Damascus road eastward, in order to visit the ancient sanctuary of Israel at Shiloh. On the way we passed a little farming village named *Turmus Aya*, situated upon a mound in the middle of the plain. The land

* Genesis 22 : 3.

seemed to be under cultivation in part, and was composed of a soil at once fertile and tillable. Soon after we turned sharply northward, rode up a gentle slope in the plain, and were at ancient Shiloh. This was one of the places which we

SEILUN (ANCIENT SHILOH).

had separated from common sites as of peculiar importance and interest. The fact that the tabernacle rested here after its long wanderings in the desert, that Joshua here divided the territory between the twelve tribes after the conquest, and that here Eli and Samuel ministered before the

Lord, gave this place a claim to our careful attention.

The first question which naturally arises in the mind of the traveller upon approaching a place like this is that of identity. Is this the real Shiloh? The position is set forth in the book of Judges as "on the north side of Bethel, on the east side of the highway that goeth up from Bethel to Shechem, and on the south of Lebonah."* Notwithstanding this clear description of Shiloh's situation in the Bible, the real site was not known from the times of Jerome until its recent discovery by an American traveller, Dr. Robinson. For centuries both Christian and Mohammedan tradition held that Mizpeh, or *Neby Samwil*, was the Shiloh of Samuel, and so its real site was completely forgotten. In June, 1838, Dr. Robinson employed a "common peasant" at *Sinjil*, who had spoken to him of a ruin northeast of that place named Seilun, to conduct him thither. Upon arriving at the place by the same route we traversed, the doctor was convinced of the truth of his previous conjecture that this was indeed the ancient Shiloh, the traces of which are seen in the similarity of the modern name Seilun.

We found the ruins of many buildings here,

* Judges 21 : 19.

lying upon the southern face of a gentle eminence, with a single terebinth tree in the foreground, near which were the remains of a mosque or synagogue. The eminence itself was really a mound separated from the higher hills surrounding it by shallow wadies, which empty their waters northward into the deeper ravine which runs westward toward Lebonah. This conformation rendered the place easy of defence, which may have been one reason why it was originally selected as the resting-place of the tabernacle and the sacred ark of the covenant. At the same time it was a secluded spot, away from the usual thoroughfare, while it was in the very heart of the country, at which all the tribes could conveniently assemble. Just before reaching the mound we came to the ruins of an old church of the Roman period, situated at the base of the higher hill to the eastward. This ruin fronted the north, and once had a large tower at its corner, fourteen by twenty-eight feet at the base, with heavy buttresses still clinging to its sides. The huge lintel was still at the doorway of the church, ornamented with the figures of a vase, and on either side of it a chaplet. Three broken columns of the Corinthian order of architecture lay within the walls amid heaps of rubbish and overgrown with weeds.

From this point we went immediately to the central mound, only five minutes distant, and, again dismounting, we ransacked the extensive ruins. As we went up the acclivity, turning from side to side in order to make our way through the ruins, we discovered that these fragments must have been used in the construction of a modern village. Bits of pottery lay scattered about here and there, and the deserted dwellings were located without any order or system in respect to streets or passage-ways. From the summit we obtained a pleasant view of the plain to the southward by which we had approached the place, while on all the other sides the high rocky, treeless hills stood like grim sentinels to guard this ancient sanctuary of Israel. Upon our descent to the single terebinth tree and the ruined mosque in the foreground we searched for some relic of the ancient city gate, but were unable to discover any trace of its location. The gate must have been near the location of the terebinth tree, for this was the only place suitable for the main entrance to the ancient city. And here it must be that poor old Eli " sat upon a seat by the wayside watching" when his heart trembled for the ark of God, which his sons Hophni and Phinehas had carried away to the battle-field of the Philistines; and here, when the sad news came that the ark of God was taken, "he fell from off the seat backward by the side of the gate, and his neck brake, and he died."* Precious memories were associated with that ark here in Shiloh, and indulgent old Eli was heartbroken even before the shock came which caused his death. Here the Lord's call came to Samuel during the silent hours of the night as they both lay within the purlieus of the holy tabernacle, and that which would cause the ears of all Israel to tingle had now come to pass. And so to this day Shiloh is desolate. Not an inhabited dwelling, not even a herdsman or shepherd, was in sight, and the prophecy of Jeremiah seemed literally fulfilled—"Go ye now unto my place which was in Shiloh, where I set my name at the first, and see what I did to it for the wickedness of my people Israel."†

Without the company of our reluctant guide, we mounted our horses and turned down the open wady to the eastward, where the waters would surely run "softly" because of the gentle inclination, and made our way toward the famous spring of Shiloh. We soon passed a number of rock-hewn tombs, with rectangular openings, sunk into the base of the adjoining hill, which, it may be, have held the remains of the descendants of

* 1 Samuel 4 : 18.   † Jeremiah 7 : 12.

the judges. We now passed into the bed of the valley, the stream of which runs on the north side of the mound westward toward Lebonah. The valley became quite narrow as we proceeded eastward, having large fragments of loose rock lying in its bed, giving it a wild and rugged appearance In fifteen minutes we turned sharply to the left, and arrived at the fountain, which is rather a well some ten feet in depth, from which a copious stream of sweet, pure water flowed into a sort of reservoir farther down the slope. This is supposed to be the spring where the maidens of Shiloh came to celebrate their annual festival by dancing, when the sons of Benjamin rushed out from the adjoining vineyards, and bore them away as wives into their own territory.*

We hastened our return to the place where we left our attendants, and followed down the stream over a rough and almost precipitous path, winding around the jagged point of rocks into the wide and fertile valley of Lebonah. Here we regained the beaten track or highway, and proceeded on our course northward. We lunched this day beneath a large and beautiful terebinth tree, and, as at *Deir Diwan*, had a number of idle men watching us, while their wives were toiling in the fields and vineyards near by.

* Judges 21 : 23.

We were now in the plain *el Mukhnah,* and our course ran north-northeast, bordered on either side by parallel ridges of blue mountains. We saw women in the fields weeding wheat, and as they plucked the weeds and grass they carried them in bundles in their arms, and deposited them at the roadside to be used as fodder for the donkeys. It was now three o'clock P.M., the sun shining fiercely, so that we almost envied the occupant of a little booth near by, composed of green boughs, which presented the appearance of a comfortable shelter. We had for the last half hour been slowly nearing the chain of mountains on our left hand, and were at half-past three o'clock at the foot of Mount Gerizim.

Here we dismounted at Jacob's Well, one of the few sites surely known to have been pressed by the feet of our Saviour. Here he sat beside the well, and instructed the Samaritan woman in the mysteries of his kingdom.* The well is situated at the foot of the mountain, on the gentle slope which sinks away into the green sward of the plain below. An old church, now fallen into ruins, marks the site, in connection with which an arch was formerly constructed covering the mouth of the well. This arch has now tumbled in, leaving a large open cavern some eight feet

* John 4 : 9–24.

in depth, in one corner of which the traces of the well appear wedged full of loose stones. It was originally very deep, but for years has been

JACOB'S WELL.

neglected, until now, at last, its mouth has become entirely filled with rubbish.*

Upon leaving this relic of ancient patriarchal life we noticed on our right the so-called tomb of Joseph,† which bears nearly the same relation to Mount Ebal that this does to Mount Gerizim. As we rode up this magnificent gateway between the two mountains, the well on one side and the ruined arch over the tomb on the other seemed to us to resemble porters' lodges, which are often found on either side of the grand entrance of

---

* See note at end of this chapter.
† Joshua 24 : 32.

some nobleman's estate. Not far away was the city to which the two disciples went to buy food, while the Saviour talked with the woman at the well.

We soon reached the two recesses, fronting each other, where the law was read under Joshua.* Regarded in any light, no more suitable place for the purpose can be found. If the priests stood in the centre of the valley, their voices could be heard at the extreme points of the recesses, while the curses could properly be pronounced from Ebal, which to this day is rocky and barren, and the blessings would come from the Gerizim side, which is covered with green trees and vegetation.†

At this point we left the line of the valley, which runs straight onward through Nablûs, and began the ascent of Gerizim. Higher and yet higher we urged our weary horses, up an ascent which to a stranger's eye seemed almost inaccessible. The merry voices of the women and children, who were enjoying a romp and swing at a picnic in an adjoining grove, rang out cheerily upon the air. After a steady and hard climb of

---

* Joshua 8 : 34.

† Joshua 8 : 33. Tristram's *Israel*, p. 152, gives an account of his party stationing themselves on the sides of the two mounts and reciting the Ten Commandments antiphonally.

fifteen minutes' length we came upon a kind of plateau, where we found a few specimens of a large flower, with bright crimson petals, of the lily or amaryllis species.

We now enjoyed a fine view of the valley spread out before us, with the village nestled against the foot of Gerizim in the distance, and the bald side of Ebal everywhere confronting us. Another fifteen-minute climb, and we were at the place where the Samaritans roast the lambs at their annual passover. The spot is marked by holes sunk into the ground and walled up with loose stones. Leaving our horses there, we continued on eastward over acres of fragments of stones, evidently employed in former times for building purposes, until at last we reached the extreme summit, overhanging the plain *el Mukhnah.*

Here we found an old tower or ruined mosque, to the top of which we made our way, and were rewarded with a magnificent view. On the north stretched the vale of Shechem, bounded by the sterile and rocky side of Ebal, with the summit of far-distant Hermon in the background; on the east was the beautiful plain *el Mukhnah,* on the south the high hills of Benjamin and Judea, and on the west, far in the distance, the blue waters of the Mediterranean Sea. With pleasure we lingered upon the beautiful scene until our guide hastened us away, lest the night should overtake us before reaching the encampment.

When we had resumed the saddle once more, we followed the crest of the mountain westward for half a mile, over loose stones, with grassy plots here and there intervening, until we arrived at a point directly opposite the village, when we commenced the descent. Half way down the mountain side we came upon the living fountains which supply Nablûs with abundance of clear, sweet water, and, amid groves of poplar and orchards of olive and fig trees, we came to our tents, ready for our use, just on the border of the village. Here, as the evening drew on, we were visited by the missionary El Karey, who, though educated in England, is a native of Palestine, and is engaged among his countrymen in the interests of Protestant Christianity. It was a pleasure to sit with him at the door of the tent, and listen to his descriptions of the surroundings of Nablûs and the character of its inhabitants. The great hindrance to his missionary work, he said, was the Mohammedan faith, which is firmly seated in the hearts of the people. The women especially suffer from this adherence to the teachings of the false prophet, which fosters polygamy and keeps the sex in ignorance and degradation. Several English ladies, travelling on horseback, stopped near a group of poor women at work in the fields, who looked with envy at their more favored sisters from a foreign land, and said, "Dismount and come and share our burdens," adding, "Surely God has blessed these strangers; they must be good women."

The question was started why the patriarch Jacob had dug that deep well just beyond the village, when the whole vale was furnished with fountains of running water. This fact El Karey explained in this way: In the time of Jacob the Shechemites had the vale in their exclusive possession, while the patriarch had purchased land in the plain of Mukhnah, which lies to the eastward. In order to avoid intercourse with the idolatrous people Jacob dug the well on his own land, that his family might not come among them to obtain water, and thus be contaminated with their idolatry. The missionary also believed that the woman whom the Saviour met at the well was a peasant woman at work in the fields, who had just come hither with her plain pitcher to get the necessary supply of water.

We found El Karey's discourse very interesting, delivered, as it was, with the true Oriental ease and deliberation. The speaker was evidently a genuine "son of the soil," and allowed the long hours of the evening to wear away while he continued his discourse, and dextrously twisted the paper of fresh cigarettes, and smoked them at frequent intervals. As he sat in the door of our tent his fine black eyes and beard, olive complexion and expansive chest showed to good advantage in the flickering light of the candle, which was placed upon the little table within, and was now burning low in its socket. The purling rills which ceaselessly flow along the narrow streets near by lent the speaker's voice a pleasing accompaniment; and when at last he arose to depart we seemed to have enjoyed the charm of an original Arabian Nights entertainment. The curtain at the tent's door was dropped, the candle extinguished, and we were soon dreaming of the wondrous tales of the Orient.

JACOB'S WELL.—As Jacob's Well is an undisputed spot, and a subject of great interest to Christian readers, we add the remarks of travellers who have recently explored the place. The fact that this is at once a relic of the patriarchal age, and a spot assuredly visited by the Saviour, gives it a special claim to consideration.

There is much uncertainty about the original depth of the well, which can be settled only by clearing it of rubbish. In 1838 Robinson found its depth to be 105 feet, Conder in 1866 found it to be 75 feet and the same in 1875, but in 1881 Rev. C. W. Barclay found it to be 67 feet deep from the top of the carved aperture or slab of stone covering the mouth. The vault of masonry built over the well is 20 feet long by 10 feet broad, rudely built and broken through at the northeast side. The vault may be the crypt of a church built over the well in the fourth century. Access to the well may be gained through this opening in the vault. A second entrance at the northwest side is walled up. A rude stone wall 4 or 5 feet high surrounds the patch of ground in which the vault and well are situated.

Lieutenant Anderson gives the following account of his descent into the well in 1866: "We lowered a candle down the well, and found the air perfectly good, and, after the usual amount of noise and talking among the workmen and idlers, I was lashed with a good rope round the waist and a loop for my feet, and lowered through the mouth of the well which we had opened, by some trusty Arabs. The sensation was novel and disagreeable. The numerous knots in the rope continued to tighten and creak, and, after having passed through the narrow mouth, I found myself suspended in a cylindrical chamber, in shape and proportion not unlike that of the barrel of a gun. The twisting of the rope caused me to revolve as I was being lowered, which produced giddiness, and there was the additional unpleasantness of vibrating from side to side and touching the sides of the well. I suddenly heard the people from the top shouting to tell me that I had reached the bottom, so that when I began to move I found myself lying on my back at the bottom of the well. Looking up at the mouth, the opening seemed like a star. It was fortunate I had been securely lashed to the rope, as I had fainted during the operation of lowering. The well is seventy-five feet deep, seven feet six inches diameter, and is lined throughout with rough masonry, as it is dug in alluvial soil. The bottom of the well was perfectly dry at this time of the year (the month of May), and covered with loose stones. There was a little pitcher lying at the bottom unbroken, and this was an evidence of there being water in the well at some seasons, as the pitcher would have been broken had it fallen upon the stones. It is probable the well was very much deeper in ancient times, for in ten years it had decreased ten feet in depth." (*Recovery of Jerusalem*, p. 362.) Lieut. Anderson made a second examination of the well in 1877.

C. W. Barclay gives some facts of interest connected with his visit in 1881. He says, "The well has been again and again described by the many writers on Palestine, and all have mentioned their disappointment that instead of finding any semblance to a well, or anything which could recall the interview of our Lord with the woman of Samaria, they have merely found a dark irregular hole amid a mass of ruins in a vaulted chamber beneath the surface of the ground. I have shared this disappointment on many previous visits to Nablûs. . . . Vainly attempting to peer into the dark hole amid heaps of stones and rubbish, we chanced to notice, a few feet from the opening, a dark crack between the stones. Fancying that it might possibly be another opening of the well, we moved some stones and earth, and soon were able to trace part of a curved aperture in a large slab of stone. . . . We cleared away more stones and earth, and soon distinguished the mouth of the well, though it was blocked by an immense mass of stone. Calling two men who were looking on to aid, with considerable labor we at length managed to remove it, and the opening of the well was clear. It is impossible to describe our feelings as we gazed down into the open well, and sat on the ledge on which, doubtless, our Saviour rested, and felt with our fingers the grooves caused by the ropes by which the water-pots were drawn up. The following day we devoted to completely excavating round the opening of the well and laying bare the massive stone which forms its mouth." It is of hard white limestone, 3 feet 9 inches long, 2 feet 7 inches in breadth, and 18 inches thick. Rev. John Mill, who resided some months in Nablûs in 1860, was informed by a priest of the Greek church that their church had bought the plot of ground, about 180 feet square, around the well from the Turkish government, paying for it from 70,000 to 100,000 piastres. He also supposes that the well is not fed by an '*Ain* or spring, but is a *Bir* or cistern, supplied by water from the surface during the rainy season. See *Survey of Western Palestine*, vol. ii. pp. 172-178.—*Ed. Am. S. S. Union.*

NABLUS (SHECHEM). Mount Gerizim on the left, Mount Ebal on the right.

CHAPTER XIII.

FROM NABLUS TO JENIN.

WE were awakened at early dawn in Nablûs by the song of the birds and the noise of villagers astir in the streets. After having partaken of breakfast we went out to examine the town. We found it quite a manufacturing centre, producing silks, cotton cloths, soap and other commodities. The population is variously estimated as between thirteen and twenty thousand inhabitants, lately on the increase; and of this number there are about six hundred and fifty Christians and Jews, and two hundred Samaritans. The others are all, nominally at least, Mohammedans.*

Evidently nature has adapted this place for the site of a city. It is in the centre of Palestine, protected from the bleak winds by the heights of Ebal and Gerizim, and is furnished with a fine mill-stream, supplied, it is said, by some eighty living springs. The valley in which Nablûs is

---

* Prof. Socin gives the population of *Nablûs* as about 13,000; the *Survey of Western Palestine* says it was stated at 13,000 in 1875; and in 1881 Mr. Falsher, the missionary, computed it at 20,760, including 160 Samaritans and 600 Christians and Jews. —*Ed. Am. S. S. Union.*

situated is only some five hundred yards in width, its bottom about eighteen hundred feet above the level of the sea, and the top of Gerizim eight hundred feet higher still.

The main street follows the line of the valley from east to west, and contains a bazaar, where a great variety of goods and products are sold. Most of the other streets cross this, and at the intersection are the smaller shops and the workstands of the artisans. Most of the streets are narrow and dark, as the houses hang over them on arches, and the two that run lengthwise in the central portion of the town are mere lanes or alleys when compared with the streets of a modern city in Europe or America. The houses are built of stone, and are of the plain pattern so common in this country, and the dress and manners of the inhabitants correspond with their shabby and dilapidated appearance.

The few Samaritans still in this their native city retain their ancient temple or synagogue. It is a small edifice, in a retired place, close to the foot of Gerizim, consisting of a square nave, with a small transept at the end facing the door, and on the left or east end a chancel, in which the ancient rolls or copies of the law are kept, with a curtain hanging before them for concealment. These rolls, which are kept in many folds of brocade and faded satins, they claim, were written by Abisha, the son of Phinehas; but Mr. Grove, an English scholar, assigns to them an antiquity of only about four hundred and fifty years.* The synagogue itself may be five or six hundred years old, and is the humble successor of the great temple whose ruins we had seen upon the summit of Gerizim. The Samaritans are probably the smallest as well as the oldest of all the existing religious sects which have any historical standing of importance. Besides this synagogue, Nablûs has four or five mosques and one Protestant mission. The great interest in Nablûs, however, is in its natural advantages and its past history. Here Abraham halted, and built his first altar upon the soil of Canaan. Here Jacob came and dug his well, and set up the altar of Jehovah; and Shechem was even then a city, so that it may be next to Damascus in antiquity, and is certainly five hundred years

---

* The age of the Samaritan MSS. is yet an open question. Mr. Grove's view is only a conjecture. The oldest MS. at *Nablûs* was believed by Dr. Rosen to have been prepared for the temple on Mount Gerizim. Dr. Davidson does not accept this view, but says its high antiquity is unquestionable, and adds, Levisohn procured a very old copy from *Nablûs* probably written not long after the commencement of the Christian era. Another codex at *Nablûs*, examined by Levisohn, Kraus and Dr. Rosen, is also assigned to the seventh century, A.D., by Davidson.—*Ed. Am. S. S. Union.*

older than Jerusalem. Shechem also became the capital after Joshua's conquest of the country. Following this was the period when the temple was built here to rival that of Jerusalem. Then followed the colonization by the king of Assyria,* through which the Samaritan people sprang into existence, with their bitter hatred of the Jews, which continues to this day. Here Jotham stood and uttered his parable,† and here at last came the world's Redeemer to proclaim the universal extent of his kingdom ‡

Of the beauty of this valley we have many testimonies. It has been compared to that of Heidelberg in Germany in respect to the sloping hillsides and abundant foliage. Dr. Clarke wrote, "There is nothing finer in all Palestine than a view of Nablûs from the heights around it." Dr. Robinson wrote, "The whole valley was filled with gardens of vegetables and orchards of all kinds of fruits, watered by fountains, which burst forth in various parts and flow westward in refreshing streams. It came upon us suddenly like a scene of fairy enchantment. We saw nothing to compare with it in all Palestine. Here, beneath the shadow of an immense mulberry tree, by the side of a purling rill, we pitched our tent for the remainder of the day

* 2 Kings 17 : 24.   † Judges 9 : 7.   ‡ John 4 : 21–24.

and the night. We rose early, awakened by the songs of nightingales and other birds, of which the gardens around us were full. There is no wilderness here." Figs, almonds, walnuts, mulberries, grapes, oranges, apricots, pomegranates, are abundant in their season.

We left Nablûs by the road leading down the valley westward, amid olive and orange orchards, where the spring birds were nest-building and making the air vocal with their songs. The millstream rippled along merrily over the shingle at our side, reminding us that this is named by the inhabitants the most musical vale in Palestine, and that not without good reasons. Many passengers, some on horseback and others on foot, passed us on the highway, besides the camels, mules and donkeys laden with cotton bales, firewood and baskets of corn husks, and, most interesting of all, a camel laden with coal-oil from America.

Our sympathy had again been aroused as we passed through the market-place in Nablûs by the sight of three young girls, from fourteen to sixteen years of age, who came staggering into the town with immense burdens of fire-wood on their heads, which they had evidently carried many miles to market. Their faces were flushed, their eyes strained as if ready to start from the sockets, and the perspiration streaming from every pore. What would we say if our own daughters were subjected to such treatment? And yet these girls, we thought, have never done any wickedness to deserve such inhuman treatment above the thousands of girls in Christian lands, who are reared in homes of luxury and blessed with every means of improvement and culture. The base system and bad government of Mohammedanism is responsible for all this wrong to humanity, and its abettors, who wink at its "peculiar institutions" in order to preserve what is known as "the balance of power in Europe," must share in the responsibility of an attempt to turn backward the wheels of the advancing chariot of a pure Christian civilization.

Another incident illustrative of Scripture came under our observation. When about one hour distant from Nablûs, we were to leave the course of the mill-stream and strike across the country toward Samaria. Just as we drew near to a fine spring by the wayside I noticed a man approaching the place from the opposite direction. He had a package of considerable weight strapped upon his shoulders, so that it would have been difficult for him to kneel down to drink and then resume an erect posture. Accordingly he came quite up to the edge of the pool, and, planting his feet wide apart, he stooped forward, and, gently dipping up the water in the palm of his hand, by a quick and dextrous motion he threw it into his mouth. This reminded us of the test which Gideon proposed in order to sift out the poor soldiers from his band. He wished for a few choice men only, whose soldierly qualities would not suffer them to lie prone upon the earth or kneel down to drink, but who were thus accustomed to take water by lapping it from the hand.*

Our course now lay almost due north, over a district full of fields of growing wheat, and studded with low hills covered with green sward, quite in contrast with the barren hill country of Judea. The distance from Shechem to Samaria is eight miles by the way of the winding valley, but our course lay more direct over the intervening hills, and thus was accomplished within two hours. We now found ourselves in a sort of basin, surrounded by hills, and in the centre of which was the oblong hill of Samaria, with steep yet accessible sides and a long flat top. On this hill is a modern village, from which two long rows of broken stone columns extend westward. We first rode up the steep ascent to the ancient structure named the Church of Saint John the

* Judges 7 : 5–7.

Baptist, dating from the middle ages. In keeping with the tradition that the Baptist suffered martyrdom here, though modern authorities agree that he was beheaded at the castle of Machærus, east of the Dead Sea, his tomb is shown in a deep cavern beneath the pavement of this structure. Evidences of former architectural beauty

RUINS OF THE COLONNADE OF SAMARIA.

still appear in the fine large arches and lancet windows in this mediæval building, with fragments of columns and capitals and traces of figures of the cross painted upon the walls. Leaving the miserable village which lies just behind the church, we rode on through the rows of columns, erected by Herod the Great as a colonnade in honor of Cæsar Augustus. They stand in two long rows, along a terrace on the southern face of the hill, sixteen yards apart continuously for a distance of one thousand yards, until they reach the western front, where a fine view is gained of the maritime plain stretching down to the Mediterranean Sea. The columns were originally sixteen feet in height and twenty-five inches in diameter. Many of them are still standing, while fragments of stone and heaps of rubbish lie scattered around their bases.*

As we returned to a point just above the modern village we came upon a spacious terrace, also occupied with standing columns, where some ancient structure had once stood, the character of which we could not decipher, probably the remains of Herod's magnificent temple. As we passed down the eastern front of the hill we noticed another group of these ancient columns located near the base at the northeast corner.

It is possible that this long winding avenue, bordered by the columns, was a consecrated ap-

* The *Survey* says: "The colonnade appears to have surrounded the hill with a cloister. The remains are most perfect on the south, where some 80 columns are standing; the width of the cloister was 60 feet, the pillars 16 feet high, 2 feet in diameter, and about 6 feet apart. On the south it extended about 2100 feet, and the remains of a gate are pointed out, and rude rock cuttings in the southwest corner, apparently the foundations of two gate towers." Vol. ii. 211.—*Ed. Am. S. S. Union.*

proach leading up to the temple. The whole hill was probably girt about by graded ways, well adapted to lend a fine effect to the imperial processions of Herod. Josephus says, "Within and about the middle of it he built a sacred place of a furlong and a half, and adorned it with all sorts of decorations, and therein erected a temple, which was illustrious on account of both its largeness and beauty. As to the elegance of the buildings, it was taken care of also, that he might leave monuments of the fineness of his taste and of his beneficence to future ages."*

Taken together, these ruins are as extensive as any remains of antiquity in Palestine, not excepting those at Jerusalem itself, or in Banias at the source of the Jordan. The first city was founded here by Omri, about 925 B.C., whose ivory palace, located upon the summit of the hill, was celebrated among the ancients. At a later date the famous siege of the Israelites by the king of Syria took place here, attended by the extreme sufferings of the besieged, until they were suddenly relieved by the flight of the enemy, which was first made known by the four lepers.† Here too was the scene of many of the acts of the prophets Elijah and Elisha, connected

---

* *Antiquities*, xv. 8, § 5.
† 2 Kings 7 : 3–9.

with the various famines in the land and the deliverances of the people.*

As we resumed our journey northward we cast many a "longing, lingering look behind" upon this battle-ground of the ages, beautiful even in its present desolation. As last seen from the summit of the high hill over which we passed, the north side of the mount appeared completely terraced, and, though evidently in a natural state, was like a piece of landscape gardening. Here and there were spots which appeared as if arranged into parterres for flowers, in curved and elliptical figures, bordered by the green sward, now in its brightest green of the spring season. It was the final triumph of nature over the decayed grandeur once wrought by the ambition and skill of our perishing race upon this "watch-mound" of past generations.†

Onward from Samaria, now named Sebaste, we had a pleasant ride through the narrow wedge-shaped territory originally set apart for the half tribe of Manasseh. The aspect of the country was not unlike that of Ephraim, which we had left behind us as we crossed the boundary line near Samaria. From hill to dale, by the side of pleasant olive orchards, along the course of me-

* 1 Kings 17 : 16.
† The name Samaria meant watch-mountain.

andering brooks, our route led us during the whole forenoon.

We dismounted in a fine orchard, filled with olive and fig trees, for luncheon at midday, and then continued on our way northward through scenery as diversified and interesting as that passed over in the morning. We now came to the long ridges, with broken passes between them, which run northward and fall away at last into the great plain of Esdraelon. This was the debatable land, where the Israelites had to contend for many years with the hordes of Bedouin, which came by the valley of Jezreel from beyond Jordan to plunder and pillage the whole district. In a sort of upland vale, the surface of which, though stony, was covered with green growing grass, we saw, situated upon a commanding summit, the strong fortress of *Sânûr*. Here, it is said, the tragedy of Judith and Holofernes took place, which is narrated at length, and with a curious mixture of truth and error, in the Apocrypha of the Old Testament.* This singular story, seldom read by the present generation, has become almost a classical legend by its frequent repetition in the paintings and statuary of the most celebrated galleries of Europe. This may be the ancient Bethulia, indeed, where the

* Judith 13 : 8.

great general of Nebuchadnezzar lost his head, and the tide of battle was turned by the fierce bravery of a woman.* At half-past four o'clock we rode over the crest of a long ridge, from which we had an excellent view of the beautiful valley of Dothan. This is the traditional site of the two wells, into one of which Joseph was thrown by his brethren, and from which they took him in order to sell him to the Midianitish merchantmen, who came from the mountains beyond Jordan, and were on their way to Egypt.† Dr. Tristram speaks of meeting here a "long caravan of mules and asses, laden, like the Ishmaelites of old, on their way from Damascus to Egypt." The tell or mound on which the ruins of Dothan are found is very large and situated at the south end of a plain of the richest pasturage, and at its southern foot is a fine spring. The remains of an ancient road, having a massive Jewish pavement, are still distinguishable here, which, taken with the fine pasturage around it, where Joseph's

* Von Raumer, Guerin, and other travellers have identified ancient Bethulia with modern *Sânûr*, but Lieut. Conder points out with much particularity that *Sânûr* fails to meet the various requisites of the description given of Bethulia in the book of Judith. He proposes to identify Bethulia with *Meseliah*, a small village about three and a half miles northeast of *Sânûr*, and which in his opinion fulfills the requirements of the ancient narrative.—*Ed. Am. S. S. Union.*

† Genesis 37 : 24–28.

brethren would find it convenient to keep their flocks, and with the fact that ancient wells are yet seen in the neighborhood, sufficiently prove the reality of the Scripture site.

Dothan is distant from Shechem about twelve miles, and is four or five miles southwest of Jenin, and separated only by a swell or two of hills from the plain of Esdraelon. The place is twice mentioned in the Old Testament account of the prophet Elisha. And its topography enables us to see how the king of Syria could station his forces so as to "compass the city," and how the mountain could appear to the prophet's servant full of horses and chariots of fire.*

From the height above Dothan we went on north by northeast, and finally descended into a narrow, stony, naked dell, not very deep, but yet sufficiently so to exclude a view of the surrounding district. It was nearly six in the evening when we reached Jenin, our camping-place for the night. This town, containing some three thousand inhabitants, chiefly Mohammedans, is situated at the mouth of the wady we had just passed through, and on the borders of the great plain of Esdraelon. It is the site of the ancient town named by Josephus as *Ginea*, and the Engannim of Josh. 19 : 21, and is now surrounded

* 2 Kings 6 : 15–17.

by rich gardens, well watered, and orange groves, guarded by hedges of prickly-pear, with here and there a palm tree towering above the houses. We found our tents pitched outside the town, adjacent to a cemetery, where we enjoyed a comfortable night's rest, without molestation of any sort.

CHAPTER XIV.

AROUND THE GREAT PLAIN OF ESDRAELON.

Our camp was early astir on Saturday morning, April 12, in preparation for our departure from Jenin. While this work of the camp men was in progress, we made a brief tour of inspection around the village. We found that the Turkish troops were in garrison here, ready to meet the Bedouin hordes who frequently, as of old, sweep over this part of the great plain of Esdraelon for the purpose of plunder upon the crops of grain and herds of cattle.

A fine reservoir, built up of masonry, is filled with a supply of excellent drinking water, which flows down from the hills over which we had come on the previous day. It is in allusion to this abundant water supply that the place is named Jenin, meaning "the fountain of gardens."

A large building, used as a barracks for the soldiers, lay just beyond the reservoir, and near by was the irregular group of dwellings in which the three thousand inhabitants dwell, surrounded by gardens of great fertility. From these a plentiful supply of cabbages, cucumbers, sweet

ZER'IN (SITE OF ANCIENT JEZREEL).

lemons, melons and dates is obtained in their season. One fine palm tree arrested our atten-

DATE-PALM. (*After Photograph.*)

tion, the most symmetrical in shape and vigorous in growth of any that we saw in the whole country.

Although this village occupies such a desirable situation, it is but casually mentioned in the Scriptures. It was apportioned to Issachar by the fourth lot drawn under the superintendence of Joshua, and in that connection is named Engannim, from which Jenin is derived, having the same signification, fountain of gardens.*

This fountain is the source of the stream which flows westward from this point, skirting the range of Carmel and emptying into the Mediterranean at Haifa, known in Scripture as "that ancient river, the river Kishon."† The mention of this title, drawn from that admirable specimen of Old Testament literature in the book of Judges, so well adapted to the purposes alike of the antiquarian and elocutionist, will afford us food for thought as we pass on our way toward the historic site of ancient Jezreel.

Once more in the saddle, we rode past the hedges of prickly-pear, or cactus, surrounding the gardens of Jenin, and took our route toward the north-northeast, across an arm of the great plain of Esdraelon. In the course of half an hour we began to cross the slight undulations formed from the spurs of Mount Gilboa, at which the plain terminates in this direction.

The name Esdraelon is the Greek equivalent for the Hebrew Jezreel, the name of the valley and site of the ancient city, so familiar to all Old Testament readers. The plain is an irregular triangle in shape, having its base at the east end, extending from Jenin to the foot of the hills be-

* Joshua 19 : 21.   † Judges 5 : 21.

low Nazareth, a distance of fourteen miles, and its apex at Haifa on the Mediterranean Sea.* The northern side, formed by the hills of Galilee, is about twelve miles, the southern, bordered by the Samaria and Carmel range, about eighteen miles, in length.

As we advanced northward the whole plain came gradually into view, and was a sight of great interest. The vast expanse spread out before us appeared to have a slightly-undulating surface, only about one-sixth of which is cultivated, the remainder being abandoned to a luxuriant growth of wild grass and thistles. The reason of this neglect is the same that hinders the work of the farmer in all Palestine—the lack of protection. From time immemorial this plain has been the scene of lawless plunder on the part of the tribes and nations dwelling to the northward and beyond the Jordan. The garrison of Turkish soldiers at Jenin is inefficient, and the government itself is but an incubus upon the native population.

Our guide informed us, as we rode along the

* The *Survey of Western Palestine* states that the plain of Esdraelon measures 14 miles north and south from *Jenin* to *Junjâr*, and 9 miles from *Lejjûn* to *Zer'in*. It has an average elevation of 200 to 250 feet above the sea level, and consists of loose volcanic soil, which is very tiring to horses and not fitted for cavalry evolutions. Vol. ii. p. 36.—*Ed. Am. S. S. Union.*

borders of the plain without a single farm-house or village to be seen upon its broad, fertile acres, that the people did not own a foot of this soil, and that for security their poor dwellings were secreted among the high hills around its borders, as in the plain of Sharon. The government owns the land and rents it out to agents (publicans), who engage to pay the authorities one-tenth—a tithe—of all its produce. The agent goes each year to the sheikh, and asks him how much his people sowed upon the land. The sheikh tries to shrink the amount, the agent to raise it. After two or three days talk they generally effect a compromise; but at the time of the harvest the grain must be left undivided until the agent arrives, often to the great damage of the crop, when he generally exacts an extortionate proportion. Is it any wonder then that the farmers here are named " poor fellows," or " fellahin " ?

Just at nine o'clock we rode up to *Zer'în* (Jezreel), a little huddle of huts standing on the site of ancient Jezreel. Poor as this place appears, perched as it is upon the barren ridge which is the foot-hill of Gilboa, it affords a commanding prospect over the vast surface of Esdraelon. An ancient marble sarcophagus attracted my attention, lying upon its side and half filled with earth, just on the border of the hamlet. It was ornamented, both at the sides and ends, with long, wavy lines separated with corrugated ridges, and evidently had been wrought in the times when this was the site of a royal city. This relic compared strictly with the condition of the few huts of Zer'in, built up of wattled grass, clay and stone, altogether wretched and dilapidated in appearance.* As we rode along the mud walls the poor inhabitants peered forth at us with blank astonishment, while the dogs as usual snarled at our horses' feet. There is a square tower of some height at the north side of the huts, partly in ruins, from the windows of which a fine view may be had of the surrounding country.

At this point we were surprised to find ourselves on the brink of a steep and somewhat rocky descent, perhaps a hundred feet in depth, running sheer down into the valley of Jezreel. The valley is broad, with its stream-bed well toward the northern side, running down toward the Jordan; opposite, in plain sight, were the heights of Little Hermon. The heights of Gilboa lay east of us, the continuation and culmination

* The *Exploration Fund* describes *Zer'in* as a village of moderate size, *built of stone*, surrounded by rocky ground. A modern tower or taller house stands in the centre of the village. The position is regarded as remarkable for its natural strength and its conspicuous appearance from the plain. Vol. ii. p. 88. —*Ed. Am. S. S. Union.*

of the ridge on which we were standing. Not a shrub or tree could be seen on their lofty summits, nor yet on their sides, rock-ribbed and barren as they were, shining under the rays of the morning sun in desolate and silent grandeur. Across the vast plain stretching far away toward the west and south flows the ancient Kishon, already mentioned, to the banks of which Sisera, captain of the host of Jabin, the Canaanitish king, was lured by the stratagem of the heroic woman Deborah, the judge and prophetess of Israel.* From the side valley, which emerges into the great plain yonder at the point of Little Hermon, in which stands Mount Tabor, the rendezvous of Israel, they swarmed forth ten thousand strong, and falling upon the rear of Sisera's army, with its nine hundred chariots of iron, routed and slaughtered his entire force.† This signal victory broke the power of the Canaanitish hostility which had continued to harass the Israelites from the days of Joshua.

Turning eastward as we stand on this lofty site of ancient Jezreel, we can see the marsh land in the bed of the valley only a mile and a half distant, where the waters of *'Ain Jalud*, Gideon's Spring, pour their strong current forth from the foot of Mount Gilboa. Here it was that Gideon

* Judges 4 : 2–7. † Judges 4 : 15, 16.

rallied his famous army against the Midianites and other children of the east, who were pouring into the country like the devastating hordes of grasshoppers for multitude, threatening to eat out the substance of the whole land.* Here he tested the men by the lapping of water from the spring, and, dismissing the great multitude, kept only the famous three hundred.† And it was in this same valley that he afterward made his famous sortie with the lamps, pitchers and trumpets, and frightened the vast host of Midianites into a rout and utter defeat.‡ Casting the eye along these heights of Gilboa, again we are reminded of the tragic end of Saul and Jonathan, which David celebrates with his noble eulogy. From this side of the valley Saul passed over on the night before the battle, and, crossing the eastern shoulder of Little Hermon, went to consult the witch of Endor as to his future.§ Endor is now named *Endôr*,|| and is but a collection of cave dwellings, shared in common by the modern witches, or women who dwell there, and cattle,

---

* Judges 6 : 3–5. † Judges 7 : 4–7.
‡ Judges 7 : 19–22. § 1 Samuel 28 : 7.

|| "It is a small village of mud cabins built against a steep hillside. A few cactus hedges exist beneath, and a small spring on the north. Above the village on the east are some small caves in the side of the hill, not ancient."—*Survey of Western Palestine*, vol. ii. p. 84.

and is more wretched and wild than the other poor hamlets in the country. It was a long journey for Saul to make after midnight, and it had a bitter and ghostly end, for he and Jonathan both perished by the sword the next day here on the heights of Gilboa.* And in the case of Jonathan, at least, all can unite in David's lament: "The beauty of Israel is slain upon thy high places: how are the mighty fallen!"†

We linger yet a moment to recall another tragedy of Old Testament history centred here at Jezreel when it was the royal residence of the wicked Ahab and Jezebel. Looking to the westward once more, we clearly trace the outlines of Mount Carmel, beyond the Kishon, where Elijah met the four hundred and fifty prophets of Baal, and challenged them to give a miraculous proof of the divine character of their religion. After their signal failure to show a sign from heaven, and the prayer of the prophet and the consuming of the sacrifice, Elijah "girded up his loins, and ran before Ahab to the entrance of Jezreel."‡ He thus ran in advance of the king's chariot, which was no doubt driven in speed, the entire distance of at least sixteen miles to this point; a wonderful feat after the fatigues of the day,

---

* 1 Samuel 31 : 1-6. † 2 Samuel 1 : 1-19.
‡ 1 Kings 18 : 46.

and performed for the purpose of showing his loyalty to Ahab's rule if he would banish idolatry from the land. But in this hope the prophet was doomed to disappointment. Jezebel's influence was paramount, and her college of four hundred and fifty priests of Baal, located here, must be sustained at all hazards. Ahab himself fell into another grievous sin in forcibly taking possession of Naboth's vineyard, situated no doubt along this hillside.* Naboth's murder became the procuring cause of the downfall of the royal lineage, for Jehu the avenger came up this valley one day and fulfilled his bloody mission.†

May it not be that this old ruined tower is the representative of the one on which the watchman stood when he spied the company of Jehu as he came, driving furiously? And these fierce dogs which prowl around the mounds where the offal is cast from the houses, may be the descendants of those which did "eat Jezebel by the wall of Jezreel." ‡

In view of the many points of historical interest centering at *Zer'in* we would gladly have remained longer, but our guide warned us that a long ride intervened between us and Nazareth, our intended camping-place for the night and the

---

* 1 Kings 21 : 7–16. † 2 Kings 9 : 24, 25, 27, 33.
‡ 1 Kings 21 : 23.

approaching Sabbath, and so we hastened our departure. We made our way, as best we could, down the hillside, reaching its foot in the bed of Jezreel, where a spring flows out, from which the villagers obtain their supply of water.

We next crossed the valley obliquely, and began the ascent of Little Hermon, now called *Jebel-Duhy*,[*] going up a gentle acclivity toward the site of ancient Shunem. We passed several small fields of wheat and barley, in which were several groups of women and girls engaged in plucking up the weeds, which they cast down among the growing grain. This brought to mind the Old Testament story, which will make the place memorable forever, of Elisha the prophet and the "great" woman of Shunem, whose son went out into these fields to his father to the reapers.[†]

As we approached the town we saw how all parts of the narrative find a ready explanation in its topography. Elisha and Gehazi would natur-

---

[*] There is, as usual in Arabic names, no uniformity of spelling for the modern name of Little Hermon. Prof. Socin writes *Jebel Dahi;* the *Survey, Neby Dûhy.* It was called Little Hermon by the crusading chroniclers, a name still known to some Nazareth Christians; and also Mount Endor in the middle ages. The hill is of volcanic origin, the summit conical, 1470 feet above the plain.—*Ed. Am. S. S. Union.*

[†] 2 Kings 4 : 18–37.

ally pass this way on their frequent journeys from Carmel to the Jordan, which led the woman to say, "I perceive that this is an holy man of God, which passes by us continually." As the family was of some distinction, "great," and as she was a person at once pious and hospitable, her proposition to her husband to "make a little chamber, and set for him there a bed, and a table, and a candlestick," was readily accomplished. It must have been a welcome shelter to the prophet when the sun was shining fiercely upon the hillside, as it was upon the day of our visit; and from the window of his little room he could look over the wide plain, quite to Carmel.

The death of the son, given to the Shunammite in answer to the prayer of Elisha, must have been by sun-stroke. The journey of the resolute mother to find the prophet for the restoration of her son can all be traced from this elevation; and so the whole narrative finds a striking illustration and explanation in the surroundings.

Shunem, or *Sôlam* as it is called now by the natives, is described by Miss Beaufort as "a little village prettily nestled in a green nook of trees at the foot of the hill." We can hardly concede as great praise as this to the place, and yet must agree that it is quite a respectable town compared with *Zer'in* and other villages in this district. The houses are very poor indeed, the children dirty, and the women engaged in bearing burdens of wood and grass, or washing the wheat preparatory to grinding it in the mill. It is thought that the heroine of Solomon's Song was from this place; if so, her successors have greatly degenerated, at least in respect to beauty of person.

Our track on leaving Shunem lay to the westward, around the shoulder of Little Hermon, with the wide plain still in view. Upon turning the angle at the extremity of the mountain we came into the side valley, which stretches down from Mount Tabor; thus we discovered that Esdraelon is divided into three smaller plains at its eastern end, separated by the ridges of Gilboa and Little Hermon.

In the middle of this northern plain we saw before us the round summit of Mount Tabor; and as we kept on skirting the mountain side, we had ample time to study its fine, mound-like appearance. In the course of a half hour's ride we came to the site of the village of Nain, where Jesus restored the widow's son to life. It seemed as if by turning around the mountain's side we had come from the territory made sacred by the events of the Old Testament, into that hallowed by the scenes of the New. But as if to warn us against the spirit of shrine-worship, we found the site quite barren, and the village wretched in its appearance. Here, beneath the shade of an old olive tree near the door of a ruined stone dwelling, our guide prepared a luncheon. While resting beneath this tree, the only one in sight upon Little Hermon, we noticed a funeral procession advancing toward the Moslem cemetery lying about a quarter of a mile to the eastward. We thought of the account given by Saint Luke of the raising of the widow's son from the bier by our Saviour;* "much people of the city was with her" we read, and truly it seemed that all the people of the village had gone with the procession that day to the burial.

It is said considerable traces still exist to prove that Nain, in former times, was a "city," with walls and gates. Now a few houses of mud and stone, with flat earth roofs, and doors three feet high, sprinkled here and there without order or system, is all that remains of this place, which was once named Nain for its pleasantness.

The sun was shining with intense brightness as we resumed our journey down the mountain side westward toward Nazareth. We crossed the plain fronting Mount Tabor near the water-shed, where the streams run severally toward the Jor-

* Luke 7 : 11–15.

dan and the Mediterranean, and after an hour's travel commenced the ascent of the hills on the north side of Esdraelon, just where the stream which flows from Nazareth makes its way into the plain through a deep gorge between two lofty peaks, where the monks locate the "Mount of Precipitation." A narrow, winding path up the steep ascent greatly taxed the energies of our already jaded horses, and it was with a sigh of relief that we paused upon the lofty summit to take a glance over the circuitous track of our day's travel. For half a mile further, amid hummocks of limestone, our trail led us northward, still at an ascending grade, until late in the afternoon we obtained our first view of the little mountain village where Jesus passed his childhood. Nestled at the foot of a lofty hill, surrounded by gardens of olive trees and cactus, Nazareth lay spread out before us, its neat houses of stone proclaiming that this was a Christian village. The clear-toned bells of the Latin and English churches were just ringing out their sweet chimes for Easter eve, and thus seemed to bid us welcome. We passed along the village street to the Fountain of the Virgin, and found our tents pitched on a gentle eminence just beyond, ready for our reception.

NAZARETH. (*After Photographs.*)

CHAPTER XV.

NAZARETH.

NAZARETH lies in an upland vale among the high hills which border the north side of Esdraelon. It is thus situated within the district of ancient Galilee. And as the great plain has always been debatable ground, separating the northern province from the main portion of Palestine, Nazareth was associated with the villages to the northward and those grouped around the Lake of Galilee. Nevertheless, this hill country of Galilee has always been an integral part of the Holy Land, the district around Nazareth having been originally allotted to the tribe of Zebulon, the portions of Naphtali and Asher lying to the north of it.

Nazareth occupies an isolated position in its little valley, surrounded by its fifteen rounded hills like "a rose enclosed in its leaves," as Quaresimus says, thus justifying the appropriateness of its name, Nazareth, *i. e.*, Separation. And yet the village may be seen from Tabor or Jezreel, or even from distant Jenin. The two rugged peaks at the mouth of its wady serve as a landmark to identify the spot, while its surrounding hills have served to defend it from the raids of the many armies which, again and again, have overrun the great plain below it. It was thus fitted to be the early home of Jesus, who spent the first thirty years of his life here, apart from the bustle, strife and tumult of the world, growing in wisdom and stature and in humble obedience to his earthly guardians. This is just as the Christian would have it; for in many respects this place is adapted for the training of a contemplative mind earnestly seeking to know the will of his heavenly Father that he might perform it.

Tradition has been busy here as usual, and the visitor is taken to see the alleged sites of the events clustering around the early life of Jesus. We were first taken to the Latin church and convent. In the former we found a high altar or choir at one side, beneath which we descended by a flight of stone steps to the chapel of the annunciation, where the constantly-burning lamps above the marble altar mark the traditional place in which the angel appeared to the Virgin Mary. Back of this we passed into a sort of cave in the native rock, named "Virgin's Kitchen." Upon leaving the church we were taken to the stone where it is said Christ once ate a meal with his disciples. The stone is about twelve by six feet in dimension, with an elevation of four feet, having a smooth, flat surface. From this point we went forward to the little Maronite chapel, near the alleged site of the ancient synagogue, which we found adorned with paintings, and containing an Arabic Bible dated A.D. 1696 and guarded as a precious relic.

A cliff just behind this chapel, some forty feet in height, may have been the place where his fellow townsmen would have cast Jesus down headlong, when with characteristic rudeness they thrust him out for preaching the truth in their synagogue.* By a clumsy tradition the monks locate this scene at the "Mount of Precipitation," overhanging the great plain at the mouth of the wady, one mile away; but this is highly improbable. The workshop of Jesus was also pointed out to us in a modern dwelling in a narrow street; but this also is without probability, for the yielding nature of the Nazareth stone assures us that all the buildings of the ancient city have long ago crumbled into ruins.

Only two objects which we visited in and about the place gave us much satisfaction. The first was the Fountain of the Virgin or "Virgin's Well," located at the northern end of the village in an open space, where the women come daily

* Luke 4 : 29.

for the necessary supply of water. An arch of rough masonry, supported by a stone wall, in the face of which several small streams issue forth, supplied by the spring under the Greek church, collecting in a deep puddle in front, is all that is now visible. Toward evening of each day the women and girls assemble here with their pitchers, awaiting their turns to fill them from the running streams, chatting meanwhile with the utmost cheerfulness and freedom. As this spring must have been the only source of supply in ancient times, it is not unlikely that the Virgin Mary used to come hither, as these women do now, to bear away water for her household, and it may be that the child Jesus often accompanied her on these lowly errands.

On two or three occasions we saw a large number of the women and girls together, and were interested to notice whether we could trace in them any feature akin to the traditional beauty of the Virgin. We found them a little superior in appearance to the women of Palestine whom we had seen in our previous travels, but could not detect the traits of "Madonna-like beauty" so frequently described by travellers. They appeared without veils, as Christian women should do, and were fairly well behaved and modest in conduct, as became their sex, but certainly were not above the average of those in their station as residents of a provincial village, either in regard to beauty of person or ordinary intelligence. Still the effect of Christian teaching was plainly apparent in them, and in years to come their descendants may have many traits of the ideal woman, their great ancestress, the Virgin Mary.

The other event of great interest to us was our ascent of the hill lying to the west of the town, and against the foot of which its buildings are located. We were favored in having a bright day, and the toil of the ascent was well repaid by the prospect from the summit. Looking northward the eye ranged over a large district of the hill country of Galilee, upon the successive ridges of which we could discern here and there a humble village. Somewhere in this part, the site now not definitely known, was Cana, where our Lord wrought his first miracle by turning water into wine at the marriage feast.* Beyond this surface of long ridges the hills mounted higher, culminating beyond the one on which Safed is situated, the city set on a hill, which cannot be hid.†

Turning to the west we saw the little seaport of *Haifa*, the blue water of the Mediterranean

* John 2 : 1. † Matthew 5 : 14.

plainly visible in its little harbor, with a vessel or two riding in the offing. Overhanging it was the bluff of Mount Carmel, with its foot pushed well out into the sea, and a roadway from the port running along its side to its lofty summit. A little to the eastward we saw the two peaks of the range which mark the place of Elijah's sacrifice, one of which had a whitish appearance, just

PLACE OF ELIJAH'S SACRIFICE.

below which was a kind of terrace with trees and green sward adapted to the prophetic tragedy. At our feet was the great plain, unrolling itself like a vast panorama, and recalling the historic incidents already mentioned, not forgetting the brilliant exploit of Napoleon, nor the earlier engagements of the Turks and Crusaders.

To the eastward we again saw the mountains of Gilboa with their bare sides, pressing their feet out into the plain at Jezreel, and beside them Little Hermon; and further to the north stood dome-shaped Tabor towering upward in its isolated symmetry, and far, far away was the "old sheikh" of the mountains, snow-capped Hermon.

A little wely crowns the summit of the hill at Nazareth, at the side of which we tarried with delighted interest, and thought that the feet of our Lord often wandered to this spot, and his eyes must have often gazed upon this lovely prospect. From this place he looked down upon his home in the humble village below, upon the great plain where the battles of ages have been fought, and upon the sea whose ships were to carry the glad and peaceful tidings of his gospel to remote lands and nations.

As our stay at Nazareth included the Easter Sabbath, we attended service in the neat edifice connected with the mission of the English church, and listened to a sermon upon Matthew 28 : 6, 7, from one of our esteemed fellow travellers, the Rev. Mr. Tyake. In the afternoon we witnessed the procession formed at the Greek church just back of the "well" or pool, where Dr. Robinson locates the spring whose waters are led by a conduit to the place of issuance. The procession passed on to the village with its chanting choir of boys, its richly-attired priests and patriarchs, with banners and other decorations, attended by a great crowd of villagers dressed in holiday attire.

The population of Nazareth is variously estimated from 5000 to 6000 souls (2000 Muslims, 2500 Greeks, 800 Latins and 100 Protestants). The number of houses would not accommodate more than 1000 people if no more densely populated than the average American village. While the materials of the houses which composed ancient Nazareth may have been changed, the forms and general aspect of the buildings cannot be now so greatly altered.

Captain Wilson when at Chorazin wrote as follows of that place: "Many of the dwelling-houses are in a tolerably perfect state, the walls being in some cases six feet high; and, as they are probably the same class of houses as that in which our Saviour dwelt, a description of them may be interesting. They are generally square, of different sizes—the largest measured was nearly thirty feet—and have one or two columns down the centre to support the roof, which appears to have been flat, as in the modern Arab houses. The walls are about two feet thick, built of masonry or of loose blocks of basalt. There is a low doorway in the centre of one of the walls, and each house has windows twelve inches high and six and a half inches wide. In one or two cases the houses were divided into four chambers."*

* *Recovery of Jerusalem*, p. 271.

As far as we noticed, the houses of the humbler citizens of Nazareth have but one room. A stationary seat runs along the side of the wall, upon which are cushions with folded quilts upon them, where the inmates sleep at night. The few dishes in daily use are kept in sight, a large clay water-jar stands at one side, and at meal times a low stool is placed in the centre of the floor, upon which a large tray is placed to answer the purpose of a dining-table.

The costumes worn by the citizens varied greatly, doubtless in consequence of Christianizing influences at work among a people once prevailingly Mohammedan. The men engaged with flocks and herds, or in the vineyards and fields, usually wear coats made of sheepskin. Those in town wear a short cloak, with a gayly-colored turban or scarf folded triangularly and thrown over the head, so as to fall over the neck and shoulders. The poorer women wear nothing but a long blue garment, tied in at the waist. Those in better circumstances wear a bonnet of red cloth, decorated with an edging or roll of silver coins. Over this a veil or shawl of coarse white or variegated cotton is thrown, hanging down to the waist. Those still more favored wear white veils, silk dresses, broad scarfs and many-colored trousers, red, green, blue and yellow. Many were thus fancifully dressed whom we saw on the occasion of their Easter festival.

The occupations of the men are quite limited, inasmuch as but little manufacturing of any sort is carried on in the village. Besides the farmers, gardeners and shepherds, Nazareth must always have had carpenters. Carpentering was the work of Joseph, the foster father of Jesus, in which he participated as a youth. The people said of him, "Is not this the carpenter's son?" And again, "Is not this the carpenter, the son of Mary?"*

Tradition affirms that Joseph was an indifferent mechanic, and if so he was engaged in such coarse work as making frames and stools, cutting poles for tents, and mending ploughs and other rude implements used in his times. His occupation would often lead him away from home into the Jewish hamlets such as Cana, Nain and even Bethsaida and Capernaum. And thither, doubtless, Jesus often accompanied him and wrought with him in his calling. When at home they had their work-bench in the narrow street.

Let us not think, however, that this humble calling left our Lord no time for worship, study and reflection. He was accustomed to attend upon the simple services of the synagogue, where he gained his knowledge of the Old Testament

* Matthew 13 : 55; Mark 6 : 3.

Scriptures, of which his deep spiritual insight revealed a new and life-like interpretation.

He was an interpreter of nature as well, and for him there were "sermons in stones, tongues in trees, books in the running brooks, and God in everything." Hence his mention of the flowers,

LILY. (*Anemone coronaria.*)   SCARLET LILY. (*Lilium chalcedonicum.*)

"Consider the lilies of the field, how they grow; they toil not, neither do they spin; and yet I say unto you, That even Solomon in all his glory was not arrayed like one of these."* Did he speak this of the bright scarlet anemones which abound over these hillsides in the spring season,

* Matthew 6 : 28, 29.

and give such beauty to the otherwise sombre landscape? Besides the anemones there are the phlox, pink and variegated; rock roses, white, yellow and cardinal; great golden flowers, pink convolvulus, marigolds, wild geraniums, red tulips, mignonnette and cyclamens. Whatever names these flowers may have had in the days of our Lord upon earth, he knew them all, and recognized in them the beauty which his Father's hand wrought in all the fair works of his creation. He also said, "Are not two sparrows sold for a farthing? and one of them shall not fall on the ground without your Father."* It is said that there are three hundred and twenty-two different kinds of birds in Palestine, and many of them are found about Nazareth. Besides the song-sparrows there are doves always flitting about and alighting upon the house-tops of the village. Upon the cactus hedges may be seen also the restless titmouse, the voluble wren and the redbreast. Swallows and swifts skim across the hill-tops, and the nightingale and song-thrush pour forth their melody when the sun is near his setting.

Familiar with this scenery from childhood, Jesus drew many of his choice illustrations from these objects, and his words seem almost to have

* Matthew 10 : 29.

a new meaning when read in the light of these surroundings. "Behold the birds of the heaven, that they sow not, neither do they reap, nor gather into barns; and your heavenly Father feedeth them."* And how fitting is his application, "Are not ye of much more value than they? Therefore be not anxious for your life, what ye shall eat, or what ye shall drink; nor yet for your body, what ye shall put on. Is not the life more than the food, and the body than the raiment?"

As the last evening of our stay in Nazareth drew on, these were our reflections. Here certainly was the home of Joseph and Mary and the workshop of the carpenter. On this hill, and the higher one westward, the feet of Jesus must have often pressed the rock or earth. His eyes took in the outline of these fifteen gently-rounded hills, which, as Dean Stanley says, "seem as if they had met to form an enclosure for this peaceful basin—they rise round it like the edge of a shell to guard it from intrusion."†

The Virgin's Well is thronged with women carrying away the water for their households in pots borne upon their heads and shoulders. The festival in the grove near by is nearly over, the children reluctantly straggling homeward. As

---

* Matthew 6 : 26 (Revision).
† *Sinai and Palestine*, p. 357.

they pass along in merry groups their clear voices ring out on the air; and the lowing of cattle and bleating of sheep passing into their folds for the night make up a scene of charming pastoral simplicity. And this is the point from which rays of heavenly light and wisdom have been spreading over the earth for centuries. From here has gone forth a faith to which the civilized nations of the world cling with ever-increasing hope and certitude as the ages roll away. For here the great Teacher of men, the Ideal of the race, the Messiah and Saviour of the world, grew up to manhood, and in his own experience laid the foundations of his gospel kingdom.

When we consider the limited advantages enjoyed by a youth who lived in this provincial village eighteen hundred years ago, and when we further note the proverbially rude character of the Nazarenes in that day, we are not surprised at the question of his fellow citizens, " From whence has this man these things ? and what wisdom is this which is given unto him, that even such mighty works are wrought by his hands ?"* In the light of all the facts of the case, is not that question fairly unanswerable, except as answered by the four evangelists and the subsequent progress of Christianity ?

* Mark 6 : 2.

MOUNT TABOR. (*After a Photograph.*)

CHAPTER XVI.

TABOR AND TIBERIAS.

WHILE we were busy with sight-seeing in Nazareth, our guide was diligently engaged in preparing for our future journey. The supply of bread brought from Jerusalem was exhausted, and a fresh stock must be laid in from the village baker's oven. It proved to be the most sodden, sour, and execrable apology for food we ever had tasted; and when, afterward, it became thoroughly dry, we thought, "When we ask bread, will he give us a stone?"

Leaving our camping-ground, near the "Well of the Virgin," on the morning of April 14, we passed over the gentle hills lying to the east of Nazareth, on our way to Mount Tabor. The morning air was cool and bracing, and our horses, refreshed by their long rest over Sunday, went forward without the usual amount of urging.

The dew lay thickly scattered upon the grass, and glistened upon the leaves of the many oak trees, which bordered our winding pathway. The country, though rather broken, was quite fertile and afforded good pasture, but only a small portion of it was under cultivation. After passing the water-shed we began the long and gradual descent to the foot of Tabor. At the point of our approach, a slight elevation joins the mountain with these hills of Nazareth, forming its only connection with the surrounding summits. The distance traversed to this point is said to be about five miles. We found the ascent of Tabor quite difficult, the trail often mounting over the projecting ledges of limestone, where a misstep might roll both horse and rider down the mountain side. We came upon many thickets of oak trees, with syringa and other shrubs, amid which wolves, wild boars, lynxes, and various reptiles have their coverts. We reached the summit at ten o'clock, having been just three hours on the way from our encampment. A fine Saracenic arch, connected with an ancient wall which formerly encircled the whole plateau, and named *Bab-el-Hawa*—" Gate of the Wind "—confronted us immediately upon reaching the level area. Passing under this, we paused to take in the southern view, which includes a section of the surface of Esdraelon. We then passed on eastward over what seemed to have been once a place for a garden, now affording fine pasture for the herd of goats kept here by the monks. The whole surface is less than a quarter of a mile long and an eighth of a mile wide, and is quite level. The height of Tabor is variously estimated at from 1000 to 1400 feet above the level of the surrounding plain, and from 1700 to 1900 feet above the level of the sea.*

At the east end of the oblong space we found the old fortress which the monks of the Greek Church have turned into a place of worship and a monastery. Here we dismounted, and giving our horses in charge of the attendants, went on to the southeast angle, where we found the remains of extensive walls and fallen columns. This is the point, doubtless, where tradition has located the scene of the Transfiguration, and these are the remains of elaborate structures once erected here in honor of it.

Had we positive Scripture evidence for locating the Transfiguration here, no more suitable place could be imagined. The isolation of the mountain, its loftiness and symmetry, the extended views afforded in every direction, and the vicinity of other places visited by Christ, would render this place most fitting as the scene of that great event. While tradition favors the theory that this is the Mount of Transfiguration, modern research de-

---

* The survey gives 1843 feet above the sea, while Prof. Socin states that its height above the table-land is about 1055 feet and above the Mediterranean Sea 2018 feet.—*Schaff's Dict. of Bible*, p. 843.

cides against it, and locates the scene on Mount Hermon, near Banias. The evangelists leave this matter of the location an open question, and probably we would do well to follow their example. The chief objection to the traditional view is that this mountain was occupied by a fortress and town in the days of Christ, and a wall, which Josephus declares that he himself rebuilt some sixty years afterward. The mention of "snow," in the evangelist's description, is also regarded as incidental proof that Hermon, which is generally covered with snow, is the mountain intended.* Dr. Thomson says, however: "The fact that there may have been a village on the top at that time does not present any difficulty. There are many secluded and densely-wooded terraces on the north and northeast sides admirably adapted to the scenes of the Transfiguration. I have been delighted to wander through some of them, and certainly regretted that my early faith in this site had been disturbed by prying critics; and, after reading all that they have advanced against the current tradition, I am not fully convinced." †

While the word Tabor does not occur in the New Testament, it is several times mentioned in the Old: first, as on the border between Issachar

---

* Mark 9 : 3.

† *Land and Book*, vol. ii. p. 139.

and Zebulun, and then as the rendezvous for Barak's army—to which allusion has already been made—and then by the Psalmist, "Tabor and Hermon shall rejoice in thy name."*

Upon returning to the monastery for our horses we hoped to see something of the institution, but the gate was closed, and as our horses were ready we mounted for the descent.†

Quite a romantic story is told of an aged monk named Erinna, who lived on Mount Tabor for many years, and died here in the year 1857. He was the son of an archimandrate of a monastery in the Crimea, and took orders at a very early age, with the expectation that he should succeed his father in authority. But soon after he had settled down in this quiet life, a vision, as he thought, appeared to him, in which he saw a

---

* Psalm 89 : 12.

† The tradition that Tabor was the scene of the Transfiguration is as old as the fourth century and as Saint Jerome. Helena built a church on the top of Tabor in 326. In the sixth century three churches are mentioned as existing then, and later a monastery. These were plundered by the Muslims in 1113, and again in 1183 by the Saracens, and a third time laid waste in 1187 by Saladin. One was partially restored but again destroyed in 1209, and a fourth erected from the ruins, which was itself destroyed in 1263. The ruins on the summit are therefore Jewish, Byzantine, Crusading and Saracenic. For in B.C. 218 Antiochus the Great founded a town on the top of the hill, and later Josephus caused it to be fortified. Tabor is mentioned eight times in the Old Testament.—*Ed. Am. S. S. Union.*

mountain of most peculiar form, and heard a voice saying, "Arise, my son, and behold thy home upon earth." The dream was repeated seven nights running, and at last the dreamer did arise. He knew not where to go to find the mountain, and no one gave him any information about it; however, he set out, and went first to Mount Athos, then to Mount Sinai, and then to Mount Ararat in Armenia; but none answered to the picture in his dream. He travelled far into the east, then into the west; eleven years of journeying, and at last he stood before Mount Tabor. "This is it," he said; "I have found it; this is the strange shape I saw in my dream; I have sought, and found nothing like this!" So he ascended the mountain, and never left it again. Here he lived for many years, and collected money from pilgrims, which, at the time of his death, amounted to enough to build the church and monastery. He is said to have been remarkable for his long beard, and for a tame panther which, like the ancient hermits, he made his constant companion. He was a man of huge physical proportions, and claimed to subsist entirely upon milk and herbs.*

* Readers of the book named *Ben Hur* will probably conclude that the author, Gen. L. Wallace, obtained the foundation for its opening chapters from the legend of the monk of Mount Tabor.

We descended the upper portion of the mountain by the usual path, and then turned away to the northeast across one of its lower ridges, and, at the distance of one mile, stopped for luncheon. We found ourselves in what western farmers would call an "oak-opening." The trees were far apart, and the ground between them was covered with green grass, variegated with many beautiful flowers. We here took our last view of Mount Tabor, which, from this point, appeared like a truncated cone, rounded off at the top. Its general features reminded me of those extensive mounds which are found at Graves' Creek, Virginia, and Miamisburg, Ohio, though much greater in its altitude and proportions; but Tabor is evidently a natural tumulus, altogether too great to have been fashioned by the hand of man.

Our course now lay toward the northeast, over a country with a slightly-undulating surface, gradually ascending as we advanced, but yet a continuation of the plain surrounding Tabor. About the middle of the afternoon we passed the khan of *Tujjar*, a place famous for robbers, but beautifully situated in a shallow wady the waters of which flow southward. As we were approaching the high table-lands which overlook Tiberias, we came in sight of the "Horns of Hattin," supposed to be the Mount of Beatitudes. This is a ridge of ground less than a quarter of a mile in length, and rising above the level of the plain over which we passed to a height of from thirty to forty feet. At either end is an elevation, or "horn," from fifty to sixty feet high, from which it takes its name. It commands an extensive view toward the north and east, as it stands upon the edge of a steep hillside bordering the lower plain of Hattin, beyond which, and at a still lower level, lies the plain of Gennesaret. The northern half of the Lake of Galilee is also in plain view from this point, beyond which may be seen the hills of the Hauran, with Mount Hermon in the distance. It is doubtless in reference to its appearance on this side that it is named a mountain, as it is only a low ridge when seen from the south. There is no certain proof that it is the place where the Saviour gave his first lengthy discourse, but its nearness to the lake villages, its lofty and isolated situation, leave it without a rival in probability or tradition. "The platform at the top is evidently suitable for the collection of a multitude, and corresponds precisely to the level place to which Christ would 'come down,' as from one of its higher horns, to address the people. Its situation is central to the peasants of the Galilean hills and the fishermen of the Galilean lake, between which it stands, and would therefore be a natural resort for Jesus, and for his disciples when they retired for solitude from the shores of the sea; and also for the crowds who assembled 'from Galilee, from Decapolis, from Jerusalem, from Judea, and from beyond Jordan.'"* Safed, which is supposed to be the "city that is set on an hill,"† is also within plain sight of this place.

It seems incongruous that a place thus hallowed as is claimed by the utterance of the "Sermon on the Mount" should be the scene of one of the fiercest and most sanguinary conflicts of the times of the Crusaders, but such is the fact recorded in history. On the 5th of July, 1187, the available forces of the Christians in Palestine were encamped upon the ridge, and "round the base of the hill on every side was the victorious army of Saladin ready for the attack." Under the burning rays of a midsummer Syrian sun, cut off from water supply until nearly perishing from heat and thirst, the Christians withstood the Mohammedans in three separate attacks, and then, breaking their ranks, gave themselves up to their fate. This unconditional surrender put the whole land under Mohammedan rule, in which condition it remains until the present time.

From this point we crossed the lofty plateau,

---

* *Sinai and Palestine*, p. 360.
† Matthew 5:14.

from which the lake can be seen to the greatest advantage, and went directly to Tiberias. While descending the long slope stretching down to the water's edge, we came upon a great army of grasshoppers, all marching up the hill and evidently on their way to the plain of Esdraelon. Language fails in attempting a description of their numbers. Every weed, every blade of grass, every stone and hummock, seemed covered with them. They were a little larger than the ordinary American grasshopper, but otherwise did not differ from it in appearance. As the prophet Jeremiah said of the soldiers of Babylon, whom he compared to these insects, they were "innumerable."[*] An immense flock of white sea-fowls, griffons or vultures, were on the track of the grasshoppers and enjoying a royal feast, to the great admiration of the poor farmers.

We rode into Tûbarîya, *i. e.*, Tiberias, through a breach made in the walls by the earthquake of January 1, 1837. This is the only town of any considerable size left on the shore of the lake, and though it appears well when seen in cuts and engravings, it is sadly uninviting to the weary traveller who is in search of food and shelter. The city wall must have been originally twenty or thirty feet in height, having tall towers at regular

[*] Jeremiah 46 : 23.

intervals, a few of which are still standing, though in a shattered condition. Many of the buildings have crevices and great gaps in the walls, and not a few appear to have been hastily thrown together, at a more recent date, from the remains of former

THE SEA OF GALILEE FROM TIBERIAS. (*After original Photograph.*)

and more elaborate structures. The population is said to be 2000,—1000 Moslems, 900 Jews and 100 Christians. But Prof. Socin in 1873 thought there were 3000 people here, more than half Jews. A tall tower, octagonal in form, with a sort of balcony fringing it around near the top, stands back toward the northwest corner of the town, and is quite a conspicuous object as seen from the surrounding shores of the lake. A dozen or two palm trees also rise above the flat-roofed buildings, attesting the former fertility of the soil and the mild nature of the climate. The houses stand quite on the water's edge, and though no traces of the city wall appear lengthwise on this side of the town, the remains of masonry may be seen extending into the water.

The effects of the great earthquake give a desolate and ragged appearance to the whole place, several hundred houses having been completely destroyed, and the great fortress on the west side utterly ruined. A few years after the catastrophe, a native stated to a companion of Dr. Robinson that he and four others were returning down the mountain west of the city in the afternoon, when the earthquake occurred. All at once the earth opened and closed again, and two of his companions disappeared. He ran home affrighted, and found that his wife, mother, and two others in the family, had perished. On digging next day where his two companions had disappeared, they were found dead in a standing posture.*

Tiberias is one of the four cities in the land regarded as holy by the Jews (Jerusalem, Hebron,

---

* Robinson: *Researches*, vol. iii. p. 255.

Safed, are the others), in which, as they say, prayer must be offered without ceasing, or the world would fall back instantly into chaos. They expect also that their Messiah, when he appears, will emerge from the waters of the lake, and, landing at Tiberias, proceed to Safed, and there establish his throne on the highest summit of Galilee. Hence the tendency for immigration to this point for people of Jewish ancestry from the various countries of Europe, especially from Poland and Russia. When their forefathers ceased their desperate, yet useless, resistance against the Roman government for possession of the country, many of their learned rabbis came to this place, among whom was Rabbi Jehuda Hakkadosh, who, about 180 A.D., compiled the famous collection of Jewish laws and traditions known by the name of the Mishna. Jewish learning still makes a show of existence here, though the teaching is carried on mainly in private houses—one would think, under many disadvantages, inasmuch as the "king of the fleas is said to hold his court at Tiberias." In addition to German, or other languages of their several countries, the Jews here speak rabbinic Hebrew and modern Arabic. Probably in no place in the world is the Hebrew spoken as a vernacular language to such an extent as here.*

* It is also spoken in Jerusalem.

We passed through the Jewish quarter, in the centre of the town and quite near the lake, but saw nothing inviting about it. The houses are square, rickety structures, built of stone, crowded up against each other without the slightest regard to order or system, and do not appear to be kept with any great degree of cleanliness. The men wore high fur caps, as no doubt was customary among their ancestors in some far-off cold climate, and beneath which their hair straggled forth in long ringlets, a solitary curl in every case dangling in front of each ear. Altogether, they looked like a people in a strange land, beset by poverty and superstition.

Having taken this casual view of the town, we entered our camp, located a few rods east of the ancient city walls, and not far from the lake shore, where we passed a comfortable night.

CHAPTER XVII.

AROUND THE LAKE OF GALILEE—THE PLAIN OF GENNESARET.

We began our first full day of observation at the Lake of Galilee by ascending the rise of ground back of Tiberias for a general view of its situation. We first noted the fact, frequently mentioned, that the lake lies in a deep basin surrounded by hills of medium height, between which a number of ravines find their way to its borders.

On the east side two such clefts in the high table-lands are noticed, named *Wady Fik* and *Wady Sêmakh*, which divide the coast-line into three similar sections. On the north the ascent of ground from the Jordan westward is more gradual, culminating in a long ridge of basaltic rock connected with the mountains of Safed, and coming out in a bluff overhanging the lake at the northwest corner. On the west and south the banks are less regular, the plain of Gennesaret having but a few feet elevation above the water-level, while two bluffs of considerable height appear, the one above and the other below Tiberias.

The Jordan flows into the lake at the northeast corner, and flows out again at the extreme southern end, through a narrow, tortuous channel. The lake is 12½ miles in length and 6¾ in

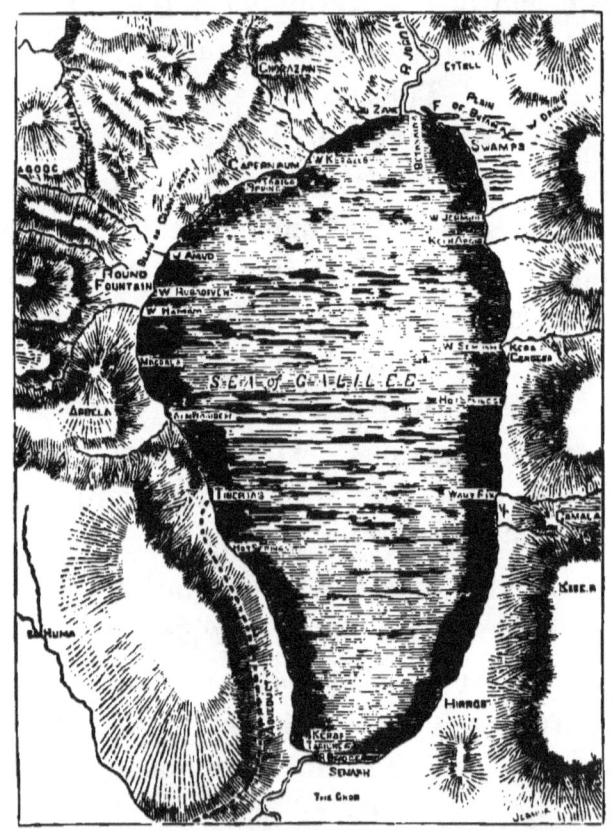

SKETCH MAP OF THE SEA OF GALILEE. (*Palestine Exploration Fund.*)

width, and is elliptical or "pear-shaped" in form. Some writers affirm that it was anciently named Chinnereth*—the "lake of the harp"—from its oval shape; yet others think that a town of this

* Numbers 34:11; Joshua 12:3; 13:27.

name once stood upon the site of Tiberias,* and that its title was changed to Gennesaret. At a later period the name Galilee—"circuit"—was given to it in connection with the hill country westward, which was originally allotted to the tribe of Naphtali; and in the days of Herod Antipas it was named "Sea of Tiberias," in honor of the emperor under whom Herod reigned. We have reference to this man in the Gospel history, for he is the Herod who was rebuked by John the Baptist for "having his brother Philip's wife," for which plainness of speech John was beheaded while in prison.† Antipas is also named the "tetrarch," *i. e.*, ruler over one-fourth of the possessions of his father, Herod the Great. Philip's portion was on the east side of the lake, including the country of Bashan as far northward as Banias, at the foot of Mount Hermon.

The two brothers were rivals, and each founded a city in his own dominions bordering upon the lake. Philip's city was situated on the fertile plain *Butiha*, at the northeast corner of the lake, and was named *Bethsaida Julias*, and was within sight of its greater rival here at Tiberias. When we were on our way to the "Warm Springs," a mile and a quarter south of our camp, we saw the ruins of this once splendid city of Antipas scat-

* Joshua 19: 35. † Matthew 14: 4–10.

tered upon the plain which lies between the high bluff of basaltic rock and the shore, of which Josephus speaks as follows: "Herod the tetrarch, who was in great favor with Tiberius, built a city of the same name at the Lake of Gennesaret. There are warm baths at a little distance from it, in a village named Emmaus." He adds that many came and inhabited this city, Galileans and strangers, some by constraint, since sepulchres were to be taken away in order to make room for the city, and the Jewish law made such inhabitants unclean for seven days.* Hence their reluctance to dwell here.

In another place Josephus mentions a "house" built here by Antipas which had the figures of living creatures in it; and also that certain Galileans set the entire palace on fire, thinking they should get a great deal of money thereby, because they saw some of the roofs gilt with gold. This, with mention of royal furniture, candlesticks of Corinthian brass, royal tables and great quantities of uncoined silver, gives us a hint of the original magnificence of the city standing here in the days of our Saviour. Probably Jesus never entered within the city proper. Though he must have often sailed along its quays, and passed behind it on the hill-top when

* *Antiquities*, xviii. 2, §3.

on his preaching tours in Galilee, yet we do not know that he ever actually entered within its walls. His spirit was more in harmony with the works of God in nature than with the bustle and din of a city whose inhabitants lived for mere sensual gratification and temporal gain. Moreover, Antipas had slain the Baptist, and his craft was compared to that of an old fox,* so that it was a matter of prudence for the Prophet of Nazareth to keep away from his haunts.

We found the traces of walls and foundations of buildings, columns, standing or prostrate, bastions or towers of masonry at the water's edge, indicating the extent of the ancient city southward beyond modern Tiberias. Near the centre of the plain we came upon a mass of ruins which marked the site of some great structure, and amid the blackened fragments of dressed stones we found three large columns of granite or syenite, of a reddish color, sixteen feet in length and two feet in diameter. Evidently there were at one time either buildings or colonnades erected at this point, to which these columns belonged. In the cliffs behind were grottoes made or enlarged by human labor, and on all sides were traces of former occupation, wealth and skill. The ruins extend nearly to the Warm Springs,

* Luke 13 : 32.

thus indicating that the ancient city was at least one mile in length, and perhaps a quarter of a mile in width. It is left to the imagination to reconstruct the famous "golden house," the stadium and forum, and the mint where the uncoined silver was stored. Evidently Antipas had the city constructed on the plan generally used by the Greeks and Romans, and was not backward in adopting their pastimes and luxuries in his court.

The morning was well advanced when two of us reached the "Springs," where the fashionable people in the days of Antipas came to bathe, and where a suburb named Emmaus was then located. At this point the bluff approaches the shore, thus terminating the plain already described. Here we noted four springs in a sort of rambling group—there are seven altogether, it is said—issuing from the base of the basaltic rock some fifty feet back, and fifteen or twenty feet higher than the margin of the lake. The first spring afforded a strong current, which ran in a rivulet to the shore, and was not utilized in any way. The next spring was strongly impregnated with sulphur, and was conducted into a square building of masonry capped with a broad dome. This is the structure usually presented in the foreground of pictures and engravings of the "sacred lake," taken from this standpoint. We entered the building, and found a round pool, once used for bathing purposes, but now out of repair. The atmosphere was almost stifling, and the water so hot that we could scarcely bear the hand in it. We next entered another and much larger building near by, where was a square tank, built of dressed stone and lined with marble, also filled with the hot mineral water, emitting a pungent vapor of gases which rendered the breathing of the visitor labored and difficult. The people of Tiberias frequent this bath as an antidote for rheumatic and other complaints. The temperature of the water is at present from 132 to 144 degrees Fahrenheit. After the earthquake of 1837 the springs became very copious, and the heat and sulphurous odors were also largely increased.

On our way from camp we had noticed that a couple of suspicious-looking characters, who had evidently been waiting at a little khan near the springs for our return, were following us in a stealthy manner. They now boldly confronted us, fiercely demanding backshish. We hastened past their rendezvous, where several armed Bedouin were breakfasting around a smouldering camp-fire. The clamor of our two assailants aroused the whole clan, and they started up as if to join in the pursuit; but as we were walking briskly, and as our camp was not far distant, they were left in the lurch, and doggedly retraced their steps, evidently disappointed and angry that their prey had escaped. As we went hastily forward, we noted the effects of the earthquake on every hand. The surface of the plain was broken and furrowed, as if a gigantic plough had been driven through it, or as if thunderbolts had fallen upon it, scattering the walls and buildings in all directions.

We did not visit the outlet of the lake, five and a half miles distant from Tiberias, where the ancient city of Tarichea once stood, now named *Kerak*. Its situation Mr. Macgregor describes as admirable for defence. "It was built on a triangular mound, about fifty feet high and four hundred yards in length, which was made into an island by the water led around it. The Jordan forms a fosse on one side, while the lake guards another, and an artificial lagoon is toward the mainland. The remains of a causeway westward from the mound show how it was approached when insulated. The desolate mound, so silent now, was once a great city, teeming with people and sounding with the shouts of the brave and the din of battering-rams."[*] This was the unhappy town and fortress taken by Titus, aided

[*] *Rob Roy*, p. 402.

by a small fleet, when the whole lake was colored with blood, and six thousand five hundred corpses were left upon its shores, while thirty thousand still more unfortunate Jews were taken captive and sold in the market-place of Corinth. From this point the Jordan continues its rushing course to the Dead Sea, some sixty miles distant in a straight line; but on account of the windings of the stream, some two hundred miles are actually traversed.

> "And far below Gennesaret's main
> Spreads many a mile of liquid plain
> (Though all seem gathered in one eager bound),
> Then narrowing cleaves yon palmy lea,
> Towards that deep sulphureous sea
> Where five proud cities lie, by one dire sentence drowned."*

Upon breaking camp near Tiberias we entered the town again, and, passing through the Jewish quarter, were reminded of the fact that the refugees slowly gathered to this point when the Romans finally overthrew their holy city and temple at Jerusalem. Here, about 180 A.D., the holy rabbi made the famous collection of Jewish laws and traditions known as the Mishna, as mentioned before. And among the numerous tombs in the vicinity, near which we may have passed in our rambles, one contains the remains of the great Maimonides.

* Keble's "Christian Year."

Arriving at the north wall, with the shattered tower at the end farthest inland, we followed its side to the water's edge, where our guide, at our earnest solicitation, had ordered the fishermen's boat to take us to Magdala. Huge blocks of stone, fallen from the walls, lay in the water, scattered about in such a way as to prevent the boat from getting within a rod of the shore. The brawny fishermen stood in the water ready to do the honors of the occasion. Their single garment—something like a smock-frock, made of coarse cotton—did not reach much below the waist, hence they were in no way inconvenienced by the flapping waves about them. They grimly seized upon us, and between two raised us in their arms, and, bearing us outward, pitched us into the craft rather unceremoniously. When all were safely on board, four of them leaped in after us, and allowed the boat to drift out into deep water. They leisurely adjusted the great clumsy oars, and, slowly drawing the prow around toward the northwest, proceeded at a snail's pace to the place of destination.

As this was the only boat we saw while around the lake, we gave it a careful inspection. It was about twenty feet in length by about five feet beam, and was propelled by three oars, the last oarsman acting as steersman, for there was no rudder. Macgregor, who is himself a sailor, says of his visit here in 1869, "The boats now used in the Lake of Galilee are all about the same size, rowing five oars, but very clumsy ones, and with a very slow stroke. Generally only three oars were in use. Their build is not on bad lines, and rather 'ship-shape,' with a flat floor; likely to be a good sea-boat, sharp and rising at both ends. The upper streak of the boat is covered with coarse canvas, which adheres to the bitumen and keeps it from sticking to the crew when they lean upon it. The waist is deep, and there are no stern-sheets, but a sort of stage aft."* Probably no great change has been made in the structure of Galilean boats from the days of the disciples; and the part here called a "stage" may be where Christ was asleep upon the pillow or boat-cushion.† These boats are sometimes driven by a sail, but more frequently propelled by the oar, and, while exceedingly clumsy, are strongly built, and in an ordinary sea quite safe.

The distance from Tiberias to Magdala is three miles, and midway between the two points a small ravine comes down from the hills and opens out into a small triangular plain at the lake shore. As our boat crept lazily around the curve of the

* *Rob Roy*, p. 348. † Mark 4 : 38.

little bay at this point, we noticed that a number of fig and nubk trees, oleanders and other shrubs grew in clumps near the water's edge. There were two round stone reservoirs which are said to be built around the three fountains named '*Ain Bârideh* ("cold spring"), formerly used for mill purposes.

The main road from Mount Tabor to Damascus comes down this wady and then follows the shore to the north side of the plain of Gennesaret. Tradition at present points out a spot in this vicinity where the multitudes were fed by the miracle of the loaves and fishes. As two separate miracles of this kind are mentioned by the evangelists, one of them may have occurred on the west shore at or near this point, though Dr. Thomson and others prefer to locate both on the eastern coast. Here indeed would be plenty of grass where the people could sit down in ranks by hundreds and by fifties; and by this route a great company might be on their way to keep the feast of the Passover at Jerusalem.* There is an early tradition of the second and also of the seventh century, given by Arculf, that '*Ain Bârideh* was the scene of the miracle, where also the five thousand "drank after they had eaten their fill." The Sinaitic version of Luke 9 : 10 and John 6 : 22, 23 places the old

---

* John 6 : 4, 5.

tradition in a more probable light, for in the former there is no mention of Bethsaida, and in the latter it is said that the place was close to Tiberias.*

However this may be, it seems that the place named Dalmanutha in the New Testament must have been near *'Ain Bârîdeh*. In Matthew 15: 39 it is said that Jesus "came into the borders of Magdala," while in Mark 8:10 we read that he "came into the regions of Dalmanutha." From this we may conclude that Dalmanutha was a town on this coast, near Magdala. Canon Tristram says that the ruins of a village and reservoirs here probably identifies the place with the Dalmanutha of the New Testament.† The identification of the long-lost site of this place is a matter of great interest both to the traveller and the Bible student.

After passing *'Ain Bârîdeh* we skirted the high bluff which forms the southern border of the plain of Gennesaret, and under its shadow we drew to the shore and disembarked at Magdala. The place is now called *Mejdel*, having only about eighty inhabitants, all Moslems, and consists of a few huts built of stone and others composed of wattled cane and rushes. A little Mohammedan mosque or wely, with a whitened dome, only in-

---

* *Recovery of Jerusalem*, p. 280.
† *Land of Israel*, p. 429.

creases the forlorn aspect of the place. This is the undisputed site of ancient Magdala, once the home of that Mary whose history is so touchingly recorded in the New Testament.*

In the face of the cliff just west of Magdala we saw the famous caverns from which, as Josephus relates,† Herod dislodged the Galilean banditti by lowering large boxes from the summit, filled with soldiers, who pulled out the desperate wretches with long hook-shaped weapons.

At Magdala we mounted our horses again—the attendants having brought them along the shore from Tiberias—and began to cross the beautiful plain of Gennesaret. We were now approaching the places forever consecrated in Christian hearts by the life and teachings of our Saviour. The names Magdala and Gennesaret recalled the matchless stories of the gospel, and seemed to transport us to the scenes of early gospel history.

The plain of Gennesaret is crescent-shaped, and is situated in the middle of the western side of the Lake of Galilee, being surrounded on three sides with high table-land and bluffs, and having a pretty strip of beach on the coast. It is three miles in length by two in depth, everywhere quite level, and elevated but a few feet above

---

* Luke 8 : 2.

† *Antiquities*, xiv. 15, § 4.

the surface of the lake. Four rivulets wander over its face, supplied from the springs and ravines to the westward, amid a tangled growth of thorny papyrus, wild mustard and nubk trees. In crossing I noticed only one little field of wheat, and another of barley, unfenced, and unpromising in appearance because of the lack of

GENNESARET, FROM KHAN MINIEH. (*From a Photograph taken for the Palestine Exploration Fund.*)

proper attention. What a contrast in appearance to its ancient beauty as described by Josephus, who says: "Its nature is wonderful as well as its beauty. Its soil is so fruitful that all sorts of trees can grow upon it, and the inhabitants, accordingly, plant all sorts of trees there: for the temperature of the air is so well mixed that it agrees very well with those several sorts; particularly walnuts, which require the coldest air, flourish there in vast plenty. One may call this the ambition of nature, where it forces those plants which are naturally enemies to one another to agree together. It is a happy conjunction of the seasons, as if every one laid claim to this country; for it not only nourishes different sorts of autumn fruits beyond men's expectations, but preserves them a great while. It supplies men with the principal fruits; with grapes and figs continually during ten months in the year, and the rest of the fruits as they become ripe, through the whole year; for, besides the good temperature of the air, it is also watered from a most fertile fountain. The people of the country call it Capernaum. Some have thought it a vein of the Nile, because it produces the fish *coracinus*, as well as that lake which is near Alexandria."

If we knew where this fountain is, we would be able to identify the site of Capernaum, where Jesus dwelt after leaving Nazareth. Various views prevail on this subject; some writers locating it at the middle of the west side of the plain, where an ancient reservoir is found, known as *'Ain Mudauwarah*, or the "round fountain." We crossed the tiny stream which flows down to the coast from this source, and examined the surroundings, but could not persuade ourselves that this could be the site of the ancient city Capernaum. We continued across the plain, stopping to gather shells on the beach, and plucking the great oleander flowers which fringed the whole coast, until we came to 'Ain el-Tin, "spring of the fig," at the foot of the bluff on the north side, where our camp was pitched for the night.

TENT LIFE.

CHAPTER XVIII.

AROUND THE LAKE OF GALILEE—BETHSAIDA AND CAPERNAUM.

From our camp at the north end of the plain of Gennesaret we entered upon one of the most interesting parts of our tour in the Holy Land. We were near the spot where our Lord uttered many of his matchless sayings, and where he did many of his "mighty works." Though no shrines or churches are erected here in commemoration of these great events, and though the exact sites of the ancient cities which once stood on this shore of the lake are unknown, yet the general locality is well known, and must ever be regarded as consecrated ground.

We first ascended the bluff which overhangs the lake, and the only one that comes quite to the shore line on the west coast, on our way northward toward *Tell Hum*. Making a little detour westward, we came to an old ruin named *Khan Minieh*, supposed to have been erected near the twelfth century for the use of travellers on their way to and from Damascus. From this point, by a sharp turn eastward, we fell into a bridle-path running along the bluff, which soon entered into a deep groove cut in the native rock, evidently used in former times as a conduit or water-course. Just below us was the famous spring, beside which stands a fig tree, from which it takes its name—*'Ain et-Tin*. It is quite a large fountain, though much smaller than *Tabighah*, on the other side of the cliff. Its waters flow into the lake only a few rods distant. A large mound on the plain near by, Dr. Robinson conjectures was the site of Capernaum; but Captain Wilson excavated it and found no signs of antiquity in its rude walls and fragments of coarse pottery.*

The rock-groove ran quite around the brow of the cliff. The groove was oval in shape, about two feet wide, and narrowed at the top,—the very least-convenient form for a road, and the very best for a water-channel. We paused under a large nubk tree on the summit of the cliff, from which a few poor women, who had been gather-

* *Recovery of Jerusalem*, p. 273. Dr. Merrill, who was here May 1, 1876, writes: "At *Khan Minieh* is a swell in the plain, in which peasants are digging, and at a depth of four to six feet they struck a finely-built wall, which they followed to a depth of twelve feet. I do not know that they reached the bottom. They traced this wall until it turned an angle, and for some distance after that. . . . If the time and necessary means were at my disposal, I would like to excavate these two low mounds."— Merrill's *East of Jordan*, p. 302. And we add, So would we.

ing fruit similar to the crab-apple, hastily departed. Their abject appearance and frightened look spoke volumes as to their hard toil and privation. As we could not speak their language, we could give them no comfort in their fears, yet could not help pitying them, and wishing for them a share in the common blessings of that gospel which their Lord, and ours, so long ago preached in this vicinity.

The view from this point was very commanding. The whole surface of the lake was spread out before us, the water deep and blue, calm and mirror-like, reflecting the outlines of the hills on its margin. Behind us lay the plain of Gennesaret, the two peaks of the Mount of Beatitudes peering up on the distant horizon. Below the plain was Magdala, and farther on Tiberias, and still farther the dome of the bath-house at the Warm Springs. On the eastern side, and nearly opposite, we noticed the wady Semakh, or Kersa, and just south of it a low bluff, steep and furrowed, the supposed site where the herd of swine ran into the sea and perished. Before us was Tabighah, with its ancient stone mill, and beyond it the cape which marks the site of *Tell Hum*.

We resumed our journey along the hillside, fronting the little bay, and presently turned eastward across the streams which flow from the

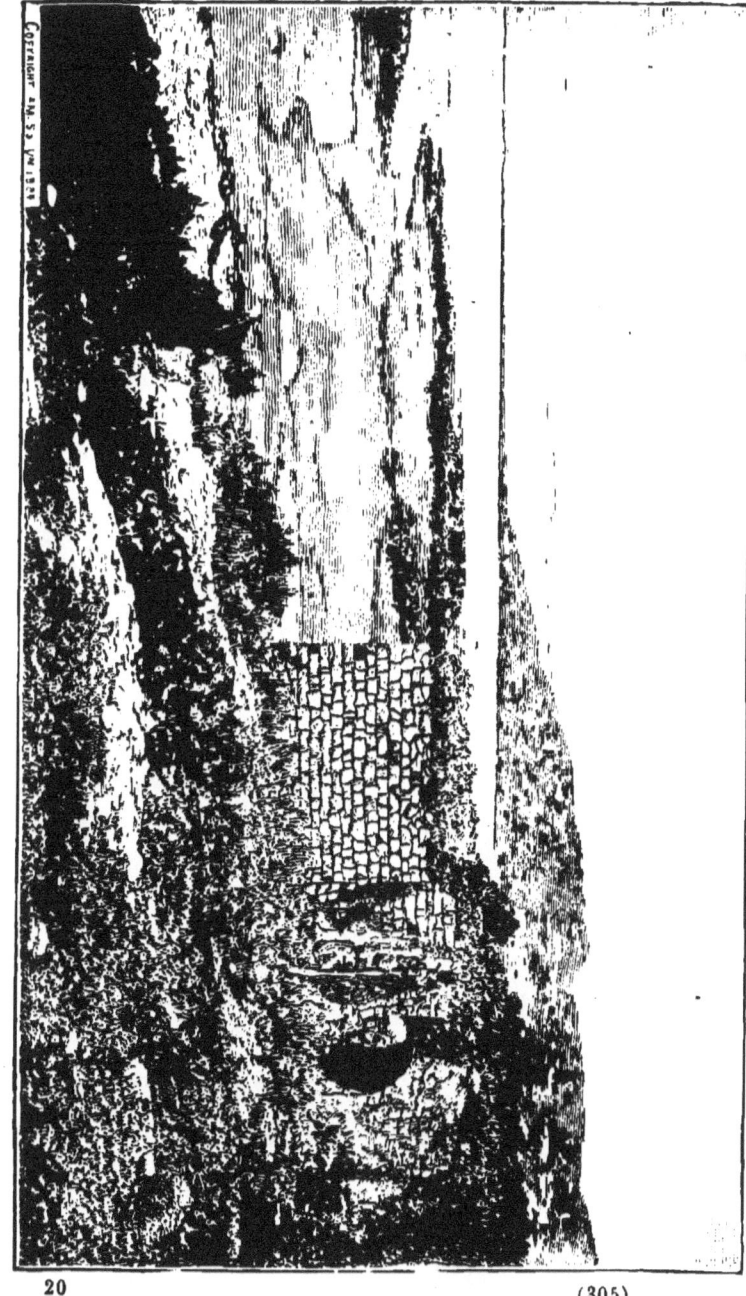

Mill at Tadighar. (*From original Photograph.*)

spring and turn the mill just mentioned. We noted a number of ruined arches which formerly spanned the mill-stream, and were part of the aqueduct which once conveyed these waters by the rock channel to Gennesaret for irrigation. Several fishermen's tents were pitched here, built of wattled rushes and covered with black camel's-hair cloth. The nets were spread out on the long shore-grass, in preparation for the following night's occupation. Several little enclosures or "fish-traps" were built of loose stones, in shallow water, within which we saw a number of good-sized fish lying with their dorsal fins out of water.

Every feature of this place seemed to us an indication that this was the ancient Bethsaida ("fish-house") so often mentioned in the Gospels. The warm water which flows in such abundance into the lake from the heavy springs above must in ancient times, as at present, have attracted great numbers of the finny tribe from the deep water to this little bay. Mr. Macgregor, when at this place in his canoe, made the following observations: "The hot springs (86½ degrees), flowing in here over these rocks, and a little farther on in larger volume over a clean brown sand, warm all the ambient shallows for a hundred feet from shore; and as much vegetable matter is brought down by the springs, and probably also insects which have fallen in, all these dainties are half cooked when they enter the lake. Evidently the fish agree to dine on these

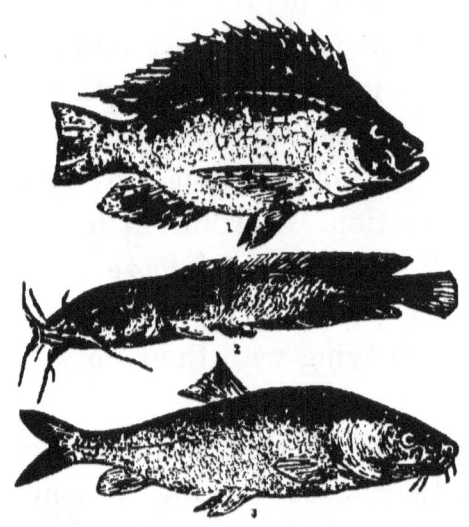

FISH OF GALILEE. (*After Tristram.*)
1. Chromis Nilotica. 2. Clarias Macracanthus. 3. Labeobarbus Canis.

hot joints, and therefore, in a large semicircle, they crowd the water by myriads round the warm river-mouth. Their backs are above the surface as they bask or tumble and jostle crowded in the water. They gambol and splash, and the calm sea, fringed by a reeking cloud of vapor, has beyond this belt of living fish a long row of cormorants feeding on the half-boiled fish, as the fish have fed on insects. I paddled along the curved line of fishes' backs and flashing tails.

Some leaped into the air, others struck my boat or paddle. Dense shoals moved in brigades as if by concert or command."* This visit was made in the month of January, hence the unusual quantity of fish and the apparent high temperature of the spring water. The fishing trade is no longer brisk as in the days of the disciples, for two reasons. First, the inhabitants are few, while in ancient times the whole district around the sea was densely populated. Josephus states that Galilee was overspread with towns and well-peopled villages. The smallest one had over fifteen hundred inhabitants. The number of towns on the lake shore, and the constant influx of travellers between the east and west and between Damascus and Egypt, made the demand for fish very pressing. The second reason for the decline of the fishing traffic here is the exorbitant tax imposed by the Turkish government. "Nominally, the rent the fishers pay for the right to fish at Bethsaida is five hundred dollars per annum; but the rapacious hands of the revenue guard carry away twenty, forty, even sixty per cent. of the fisher's hard-earned gains."

Mr. Macgregor, who is our authority for this statement, found three fishing-boats in and about the lake in 1869; but travellers who have been

* *Rob Roy*, p. 336.

here at intervals for fifty years, like the writer, have noticed but one.

Leaving Tabighah, we continued on our course in a northeast direction. In this part the land slopes back from the shore uniformly and gently to the higher hills extending up toward Safed. After a ride of one and a half miles, we reached

RUINS AT TELL HUM. (*From a Photograph. Palestine Exploration Fund.*) *From Schaff's Dictionary, by permission.*

the ruins of *Tell Hum*, where we dismounted and spent a considerable time in exploration. The ruins are partly basaltic and partly limestone fragments, once dressed and fitted into structures of no common order. Long grass and thistles were already springing up among them in April, thus showing that the climate is warm and the soil fertile. A little cape projects into the lake at this point, and the ruins lie about one hundred yards from the water. They are two miles distant from the entrance of the Jordan into the lake, and thus the town had a prominent, as well as central, position on the northern coast.

The greater portion of the ruins seems to lie in a narrow belt, half a mile in length by a quarter of a mile in breadth, with the longer axis north and south, stretching back from the shore. At the farther end are two tombs, built of limestone, of fine workmanship. In the midst of these fallen walls, which seem to be mainly the fragments of former dwellings, we came upon what is known as the "White Synagogue"—thus named under the supposition that *Tell Hum* is indeed the long-lost site of Capernaum, and this the synagogue in which Christ preached the sermon on the "bread of life," recorded in the sixth chapter of the Gospel of St. John. If so, the structure may represent the one originally built by the Roman centurion.* Here we noticed the foundations of the outer walls *in situ*, level with the surface, but happily left bare by the excavations of the Palestine Exploration Fund. They are 74 feet 9 inches by 56 feet 9 inches in dimensions. A smaller structure, and of apparently later construction, joins the main edifice on the northeast corner; we could not trace its complete outline.

We counted the pedestals of some thirty col-

* Luke 7 : 4, 5.

umns in the synagogue, the shafts of which lay broken around them. Two rows of these columns once ran lengthwise, dividing the edifice proportionately, as if there had been two aisles at the side, with a nave in the centre. The front was toward the south, overlooking the lake and commanding a charming prospect, reaching to Tiberias in the distance. Here lay the heavy lintel, pierced with large holes at either end for the extended framework of the heavy double doors to turn in, and one for the standard in the centre. On the face of this stone beam or lintel three figures were engraved,—somewhat defaced, but apparently representing a pot of manna and two golden candlesticks. Not far from the entrance a flight of stone steps, much worn, was seen, imbedded in the earth, the use of which we could not determine.

Just east of *Tell Hum* a little rivulet makes its way into the lake, on the banks of which, one and a half miles to the north in a direct line, lie the supposed ruins of Chorazin, now named *Kerazeh*. This place we did not visit; but the ruins are described as covering an area equal to, if not larger than, the ruins of Capernaum, and are situated partly in a shallow valley, partly on a rocky spur formed by a sharp bend in the stream, here a wild gorge eighty feet deep. From

Kerazeh there is a beautiful view of the lake to its southern end, and here too are gathered the most interesting ruins—a synagogue, with Corinthian capitals, niche heads and other ornaments cut in the hard basaltic rock.*

Our visit inclined us to favor *Tell Hum* as the site of ancient Capernaum. Though great authorities differ from this view, fixing the site of this city where Jesus had his home during the three years of his ministry elsewhere, or else leaving the whole matter an open question, yet the conclusion seemed to us irresistible. Captain Wilson affirms, in behalf of the Exploration Fund, that the ruins here are of a synagogue similar to many found and carefully examined in other parts of the country.

At the corners of a triangle, therefore, whose sides measure one and one-half miles each, whose base is on the shore line, and whose apex is on the hillside, probably lay ancient Chorazin, Bethsaida and Capernaum.

As we sat upon the prostrate columns of the synagogue the Saviour's words flashed upon us with a new meaning—"Woe unto thee, Chorazin! woe unto thee, Bethsaida! for if the mighty works had been done in Tyre and Sidon which have been done in you, they had a great while

* *Recovery of Jerusalem*, p. 270.

ago repented, sitting in sackcloth and ashes. But it shall be more tolerable for Tyre and Sidon at the judgment than for you. And thou, Capernaum, which art exalted to heaven, shalt be thrust down to hell."

> " Bethsaida, where ?
> Chorazin, where art thou ?
> His tent the wild Arab pitches there,
> The wild reeds shade thy brow.
> Tell me, ye mouldering fragments, tell,
> Was the Saviour's city here ?
> Lifted to heaven, has it sunk to hell,
> With none to shed a tear ?"

How signally has that prophecy been fulfilled! Where was once a tide of human prosperity, a city of fame and beauty by the sea, are now only fragments of rock, covered by rank weeds and thistles.

On our way back to Tabighah we thought of those words of Isaiah quoted by Saint Matthew —" The land of Zabulon, and the land of Nephthalim, by the way of the sea beyond Jordan, Galilee of the Gentiles."* This great highway of ancient times, running from Egypt to the East, came down here " by the way of the sea," and here it may literally be said, " The people which sat in darkness saw great light."† Along this " way " Jesus often came if, indeed, as we think,

---

* Matthew 4 : 15. † *Ibid.* 4 : 16.

Tell Hum was Capernaum and Tabighah was Bethsaida. The latter place was the suburb and port of Capernaum, and this mile and a half was familiar ground to the disciples and their divine Master. Here the fishers kept their boats and nets and plied their craft, while on some occasions their Lord taught the people from the ship. To this point the boat would return, to "his own country," when the various voyages across the lake were ended. These low lands are calculated to breed fevers, of which Peter's wife's mother lay sick, and of which she was cured by a touch of the great Physician. Yonder hillside would afford the natural features for the parable of the sower, where the ledge of rock covered with a thin coating of soil, in which the seed would have no depth of earth, and soon wither away, illustrates the failure of a transient faith. Below the rock is the good ground where the good seed would bring forth some thirty, some sixty and some an hundred fold; and above the unfenced field are the numerous birds, ready to catch away the exposed seed, and thus disappoint the farmer. Nor are the rank thistles and thorns lacking near the shore, ready to choke the growing grain and render it unfruitful.

Here also would be the natural place for a tax-gatherer, like Matthew, sitting at the receipt of custom, collecting for the Roman government. This fountain at Tabighah might very well be that named Capernaum by Josephus, since it is located in this suburb of that city, and would naturally be mentioned by him in connection with Gennesaret, since the aqueduct at that time conducted its waters into that plain for purposes of irrigation. The walls of the ancient reservoir are still to be seen just above the mill, from which point the aqueduct extended. The *coracinus* (catfish) is found in the stream all through the winter season.

Passing along the rock channel over the bluff, it occurred to us that the channel was probably covered over in ancient times, thus affording a roadway on its surface. The road which we followed from Solomon's Pools to Bethlehem was constructed precisely in this manner, and we there heard the water gurgling beneath the flagstones upon which our horses walked. If this conjecture be correct, Jesus must have often passed here on his way to and from the plain and the hill country of Galilee.

Our last evening in camp at *'Ain et-Tin* was delightfully tranquil. The waters of the lake lay spread out before us in charming repose. The rays of the setting sun lighted up the eastern shore with a soft radiance as the shadows fell around us on Gennesaret. Gathering at the door of the tent, we sang a number of our Sunday-school hymns, during which the following lines of Dr. Morris came up in recollection:

> "Each cooing dove and sighing bough,
>   That makes the eve so blest to me,
> Has something far diviner now:
>   It bears me back to Galilee.
>
> "Each flow'ry glen and mossy dell,
>   Where happy birds in song agree,
> Through sunny morn the praises tell
>   Of sights and sounds in Galilee.
>
> "And when I read the thrilling lore
>   Of him who walked upon the sea,
> I long, oh how I long once more
>   To follow him in Galilee.
>
> "O Galilee! sweet Galilee!
>   Where Jesus loved so much to be;
> O Galilee! blue Galilee!
>   Come sing thy song again to me!"

The old rabbins had a saying, "I have created seven seas, saith the Lord, but out of them all I have chosen none but the sea of Gennesaret." If this sheet of water was thus honored by the Jews, it should be thrice precious to Christian hearts, for on its shores the great Founder of Christianity not only had his earthly home, but it was here that he called together his disciples and organized his Church. This is the birthplace of Christianity. In the hearts of the humble fishermen and the poor women who dwelt here, to whom his true character was first revealed, he founded his gospel kingdom, and from hence it is spreading over the whole earth. Hence our lasting interest in this place.

> "How pleasant to me thy deep blue wave,
>   O Sea of Galilee!
> For the glorious One who came to save
>   Hath often stood by thee.
>
> "Graceful around thee the mountains meet,
>   Thou calm reposing sea;
> But ah! far more, the beautiful feet
>   Of Jesus walked o'er thee.
>
> "O Saviour! gone to God's right hand,
>   Yet the same Saviour still,
> Graved on thy heart is this lovely strand,
>   And every fragrant hill."—*M'Cheyne.*

CHAPTER XIX.

THE VALLEY OF THE HULEH.

The morning of our departure from the plain of Gennesaret was bright and beautiful. Our tents formed a group of white mounds near the pretty little beach along the lake shore, having the dark basaltic bluff above '*Ain et-Tin* for a background. Clumps of cane, nubk trees and blooming oleanders were scattered over the surface of the plain in wild and luxuriant growth, with here and there open glades between, in one of which our camp was situated.

Across the lake, from whence we had watched the last rays of the setting sun fade away the evening before, we now saw the spreading beams of the sunrise gilding the sides of the sombre hills, and peering over into the tranquil water below. Flocks of white pelicans, gray king-fishers and turtle-doves of varied plumage whirled past us on their way from Wady Hamam ("ravine of pigeons"), which bounds the plain on the south near Arbela and Hattin, to the fish shoals and cane-brake at Tabighah in quest of an early breakfast.

Taking the hint from these provident birds, and with an eye to the coming labors of the day, we entered the dining tent, and perched upon camp-stools around the table discussed the merits of the lake fish, which our cook had thoughtfully provided as the principal dish of our meal. We found the fish palatable, but the grain seemed rather coarse and the flavor rather negative. Canon Tristram has an interesting remark regarding the lake fish, affirming that of the ten species obtained by him here all were African or of a tropical genus which has never been found farther north than the Jordan and the Sea of Galilee. Upon which he puts this significant question, "Do not these most interesting and unexpected discoveries point to some ancient geological epoch, when the long chain of fresh-water lakes extended from Hermon to the Zambesi, and the Jordan was an African river flowing into the Dead Sea, then a lake connected with the African lakes by the Red Sea, also a lake?"* This startling theory is more than matched by a French savant, M. Lortet, who claims to have found forty-two different kinds of fish in the lake, and who thinks that at one time the salinity of these waters equalled that of the Dead Sea. It has been suggested by some of M. Lortet's countrymen, who

* *Land of Israel*, p. 580.

are getting famous in feats of engineering, that a canal could be cut from Haifa to Zerin, across the plain of Esdraelon, by which the valley of the Jordan could be filled with water, and the surface of this lake raised over 600 feet, while 1300 feet would be added to the depth of the Dead Sea, causing the water to flow through the Arabah to the Elanitic Gulf. What advantage would follow from this we cannot foresee; but all lovers of biblical sites would regret to hear that Jericho and Gennesaret had been submerged in order to bring the surface of these waters up to the sea level.

Having dispatched the fish breakfast and these associated water theories, we prepared ourselves for the forenoon ride to the valley of the Huleh. Our route led us past Khan Minieh, up the steep hillside, along a tortuous path bordered by loose basaltic rocks. An hour's travel brought us abreast a huge mass of scoria crowning a slight elevation, in appearance like the crater of an extinct volcano. From this elevation the high ridge of black rock runs down directly to the lake at 'Ain et-Tin, and seems to have been formed by volcanic agency at this point in some remote geological age. As we continued our course in a northwesterly direction, we passed through a region of high table-land, the surface of which was literally covered with huge fragments of the basaltic stone, amid which our horses found great difficulty in getting a firm foothold. Having arrived at the summit at about nine o'clock, our guide ordered a halt, and turning in his saddle bade us take our parting view of the Lake of Galilee.

We were now in the neighborhood of Safed, and were favored with a prospect for which this "city set upon a hill" must ever be famous. Far away to the south we traced the route by which we had approached the sacred lake, indicated by the well-defined outlines of Tabor and the Horns of Hattin. And just below us, but sunk in its deep basin, its surface burnished by the sun's rays till it looked like a mirror of molten metal, was the remarkable sheet of water on whose shores we had been delighted to tarry for the past few days. We could dimly discern the city of Tiberias, the cliff of Arbela, and on the farther side the cliffs bordering wadies Fik and Semakh.

Soon after leaving this point, from whence the little streams which flow past Tabighah and Tell Hum take their rise, and which cannot be far distant from the ruins now affirmed to be Chorazin, we came to *Khan Yûsef*. Here we found the ruins of a large stone structure, built in the form of a parallelogram, or hollow square, with a tower at one corner and a gateway on the north side. We rode through the ancient and lofty portal, and found ourselves within a spacious court, around which were the alcoves or rooms originally arranged for the accommodation of travellers. It would require but a slight expense to refit this khan for its intended use, as the walls are yet quite perfect.

The structure is evidently of Mohammedan origin, and must have been constructed at a comparatively recent period. The tradition which fixes the name also affirms that Joseph lived and died in the holy city of Safed, which is in the centre of this region. Of course, the well of Dothan, into which the cruel brethren cast the unsuspecting Joseph, is pointed out near by, though all Christian authorities fix its site south of Esdraelon. The "Bridge of the Daughters of Jacob," which spans the Jordan not far from this place, has the same authority for its name, viz., Mohammedan tradition.

The fact that such improbable traditions are attached by the Mohammedans to all the historic sites in Palestine is significant. The religion of nearly all the country people is Mohammedan, and it does but little for them in the way of enlightenment and culture. They generally hold, our guide informed us, that Abram, Jacob, Moses and Jesus were of like faith with themselves. And they further imagine that these personages were all great giants, from eight to ten feet in height, and physically strong in proportion. One week later, while traversing the great Lebanon valley, we came upon the alleged tomb of Noah,

LAKE HULEH, OR WATERS OF MEROM, FROM THE SOUTHWEST. (*From Schaff's Dictionary, by permission.*)

which was three feet wide and ninety feet in length, from which we inferred that Noah must be a great saint in the Moslem calendar.

Beyond *Khan Yûsef* the land slopes down toward the bed of the upper Jordan, now named the valley of the Huleh. In this region we passed over several plateaus, evidently covered with a fertile soil, part of which was under cultivation. In one place we passed a group of farmers at work, and were reminded of the history of Elisha. Twelve yoke of oxen were following each other in a line, each drawing a separate plough of the

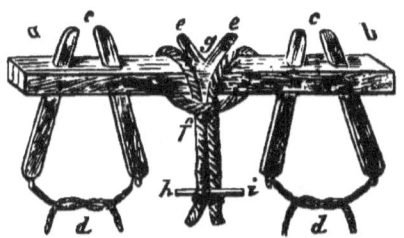

YOKE IN USE IN PALESTINE.

a, b, timber of the yoke; *c, d*, the bows; *e, e*, pegs between which, at *g*, the end of the shaft comes, the shaft itself having been run through the rope between *f* and the cross-piece of wood *h, i*. (*From Schaff's Dictionary, by permission.*)

primitive pattern already described in the account of our tour to Hebron. From the Scripture narrative it appears that Abel-Meholah, the "meadow of the dance," where Elisha was at work, was somewhere in the Jordan valley. Elijah was on his way from Sinai to Damascus, and might have come upon Elisha somewhere near this place. Custom changes so little in the lapse of centuries in this strange land that these ploughmen may be the literal successors of Elisha. He "was ploughing with twelve yoke of oxen before him, and he with the twelfth: and Elijah passed by him, and cast his mantle upon him."[*]

[*] 1 Kings 19 : 19.

He was at the rear of the line, and therefore his parley with Elijah would not hinder the other ploughmen who preceded him in their work. We again noted the truth of the statement that the farmers' little ploughs make no proper furrows, but merely "root up" the soil on either side, and so any number may follow one another, each making its own scratch along the surface of the earth, and when at the end of the field they can return along the same line, and thus back and forth until the whole is ploughed. It was well, therefore, that Elisha came last, for the ploughmen cannot pass one another, and his interview with Elijah was the more private and did not stop the others until they reached the end of the furrow. During our morning ride we had been in sight of the waters of Merom, Lake Huleh, a body of water not unlike the Lake of Galilee in shape, but of less depth and smaller dimensions.

Midday was upon us when we entered the Jordan valley once more, at a point where a mill-stream flows into the lake at its northwest extremity. The sun was now shining "in his strength," and our thirsty horses pressed into the water at the ford, drinking and splashing the swift-flowing current without regard to the convenience of the riders. The place is named *'Ain el-Mellaha*, "The Salt," or, as other authorities affirm, "spring of the king," in allusion to Joshua's victory here over Jabin.* Our guide directed us to the scanty shade of a terebinth tree, standing well up against the hillside on the north bank of the stream, where he decided that we should have a brief rest and partake of luncheon.

Our resting-place overlooked the ford, and was in plain sight of a rude mill which stood above it, with its simple machinery in motion. A number of horses, camels and donkeys were disporting themselves in the running water, and a herd of buffaloes were wallowing in the deep water farther down, where a sort of lagoon is formed by the not-distant lake. The young herdsmen were sharing the luxury of a bath with their cattle, after which they sheltered themselves beneath a clump of alders on the bank, and regaled themselves with music from a reed flute, evidently of their own invention and manufacture.

The original name of the lake was the Hebrew Merom, or "High Lake," but in the days of the Crusades it was known by the present title "Huleh," depression. The latter title probably applied to the whole valley as a hollow among the hills, while Merom indicates the lake proper as "high" among the waters.

Dean Stanley gives the dimensions of the lake

* Joshua 11 : 5.

as about seven miles long, and in its greatest width six miles wide. But Mr. Macgregor, who explored its banks in his canoe, states that according to his observation the size of the lake is not one-fourth of this area. A late writer gives the length as four miles and the breadth three and a half, having a depth of eleven feet in winter, the surface nearly on a level with the sea. It is of triangular shape, having the base at the north end, and the apex at the outlet on the south. On its western shore below *'Ain Mellaha* are excellent wheat fields, though poorly cultivated, and on its north side are acres of marsh covered with Egyptian papyrus.

The heat was very intense during our afternoon journey northward along the border of the great marsh, with scarcely a breath of air to relieve the sultry, fever-laden atmosphere. On our left hand ran a range of treeless hills, under the shadow of which we crept along, seeking there a partial shelter from the scorching rays of the sun. Great herds of buffaloes wallowed in the marsh, content to have only their eyes and nostrils exposed to the swarms of flies and mosquitoes. I counted seventy-five in one herd, and we were scarcely out of sight of them during the whole afternoon.*

---

* St. Willibald, of the eighth century, writes: " Armenta mirabilia longo dorso, brevibus cruribus, magnis cornibus creati;

At intervals we came upon encampments of the Ghawarineh people, who own the buffaloes, and for the most part gain their subsistence from them. They seldom kill them for food, for they only eat a small quantity of meat, and that for the most part mutton; though, if a buffalo break a leg and they must kill it, they sometimes eat the flesh. At certain seasons of the year the people move their camps back to Kades, two miles distant among the high hills to the westward. This is the ancient Kedesh, in the tribe of Naphtali, originally appointed as one of the cities of refuge.* There are many ruins of buildings at Kades, but none yet discovered are of great importance. Our guide informed us that the people pass the winters in their rush tents with camel's-hair covering, subsisting for the most part on coarse bread, milk and curds, rice and other simple articles of food, obtained usually from Safed or Damascus.

Late in the afternoon we arrived at another stream of water, flowing into the marsh on its west side, named *'Ain Belata,* where we pitched our camp for the night, and snatched a little time

---

omnes sunt unius coloris," *i. e.,* " extraordinary cattle, furnished with long backs, short legs and great horns; all are of one color."

* Joshua 20 : 7.

for making records of the day's observations. At this point the range of hills comes boldly out into the valley, and assumes quite a majestic appearance. The plain is here quite narrow, being hemmed in by the encroaching marsh, covered with a growth of papyrus and cane, through which the tough-skinned buffalo even cannot make his way. In this narrow plain our tents were pitched on the green sward, and we prepared for a good night's rest beneath their shelter.

During the early evening there was a strange rumbling along the side of the mountain overhanging us. Puffs of heated air eddied round the camp, and might have been taken by us as warnings of the approaching sirocco; but we were weary with travel, and early sought our tent beds without making any defence against the oncoming tempest. About ten o'clock the wind suddenly increased in violence. The storm came bellowing along the mountain side, and swooped down upon us with great force. Amid the roaring blast cries were heard for help, and upon going to the tent door we found our good neighbors and fellow travellers, the three English clergymen, without a shelter, and their clothing and valuables scattered about amid the debris of the overturned tent.

With great ado, and after much talk and bluster, our twelve camp men re-erected the fallen tent. The weary, but now apprehensive, travellers gathered up their clothing and valuables and returned to their narrow beds. Just then a terrific blast came down the mountain side, and away went *our* tent, cords, centre-pole and all the appliances, and we were left under the open heavens, while a hot blast as from the mouth of a furnace swept over us. Upon lighting one of the camp lanterns it was found that four out of our five tents were prostrate.

Now ensued a scene of aimless effort and linguistic confusion. Men were straining at tent-cords, bracing the centre-poles, driving the tent-pins in the soft ground, while the wind and the gush of Arabic speech produced a perfect Babel. During a lull in the storm we once more entered the re-erected tent, when suddenly the wind charged upon us with renewed violence. I felt the tent moving again, and grasping the centre-pole quickly blew out the candle, and was flung directly across my bed, the heavy weight of the "pole" crushing it to the ground. It was one o'clock A.M. before the wind died away sufficiently to allow us to lie down in quietness, and it was but little sleep that we obtained throughout the whole night.

CHAPTER XX.

DAN AND BANIAS.

The morning of April 17 dawned upon our company of weary pilgrims in the valley of the Huleh. Our night's experience with the sirocco was calculated to render us dissatisfied with the latest phase of tent and saddle life; but each one seemed to regard the matter in the light of an adventure common to this mode of travel, and so good humor and cheerfulness reigned supreme. The various aspects of the occurrence were jocularly canvassed at the breakfast table, and in good season we were all prepared for the journey of another day. A brief description of the nomadic life which, like the ancient patriarchs, we passed in the "promised land" may be of interest in connection with what has just been narrated. Allusions have already been made to the fact that a few tourists in the Holy Land have to secure the services of a large number of servants and horses, in order to pass through the country with safety and comfort. In our case there were only nine travellers on the long tour from Jerusalem, and yet we required twelve men and thirty animals to transport us.

The method of progress was as follows: When about breaking camp in the morning the horses, mules and donkeys were supplied with beans and barley mixed with chaff. This was placed in a sort of canvas bucket, known as the "nose-bag," the bale of which was fastened over the animal's head back of the ears. While the process of grooming, harnessing or saddling went forward, the animals munched this dry breakfast, glancing wearily meanwhile at the busy preparations going forward around them, their eyes just visible above the rim of their portable mangers. At the same time, in another part of the camp, where the kitchen tent was pitched, the cook was preparing coffee and broiling steaks or cutlets over a tin range, in which a charcoal fire was kindled; and at still another point two men were taking down the sleeping-tents and rolling them up in large packages ready for transportation. While the tourists were at breakfast the camp men (who had previously eaten at the kitchen tent) would load the tent-poles, the canvas, the huge chests of oranges and other provisions on the sumpter-mules; and while the travellers were strapping their water-proofs, etc., and getting into the saddles, the men would pull down the kitchen and dining-tents, and in an incredibly short time be upon the road *en route* to the next station.

Not a breath of air was stirring as we slowly moved up the valley from 'Ain Belata. The sun was shining intensely bright, and the buffaloes, as usual, were lazily immersing themselves in the muddy water of the marsh. The rank growth of papyrus still continued, with no visible trace of the Jordan, which makes its way somewhere through the dense jungle. Mr. Macgregor attempted to force a passage through from the north with his canoe Rob Roy, in 1869, but failed. Upon going overland to 'Ain Mellaha he launched upon Lake Huleh, and explored a narrow channel upward, for some three miles, to a point near 'Ain Belata, where he entered a little lake half a mile in width, quite surrounded by the tall green papyrus except at the south, where he had entered. He was satisfied that this is the earliest flow of Jordan as one river after it dives into the barrier, which he describes as a dense hedge of a curious floating forest. If it were desired, an open water-way could be made by cutting out the spongy bed of fallen cane and living fibre for a half-mile or more, when the Jordan would be traceable from its source to its mouth.

During the morning's ride we passed the largest village of rush tents, with black goat-hair-cloth covering, we had yet seen. Naked children were playing about the tent doors, one of which called out to us "Good morning"—a bit of English he kept repeating in great glee, having heard it, no doubt, from previous tourists who had passed that way. Near by a young woman was pounding wheat with a mallet on a large boulder; and we also saw several hand-mills, consisting of

WOMEN GRINDING AT THE MILL IN THE EAST.

the upper and nether stones of circular form, with their flat surfaces in contact, in the former of which a wooden pin was inserted, to be used as a handle in turning. Two women usually sit, one on either side of the apparatus, the one turning the stone half way around, and the other then grasping the handle to complete the revolution. This is the "mill" often mentioned in the Bible.*

* Ecclesiastes 12:4; Matthew 24:41.

At nine o'clock we saw the supposed site of ancient Hazor, "enclosure" or "castle," the possession of King Jabin in the days of Joshua,[*] situated on a rocky eminence, overlooking Kades and Lake Huleh. We had now arrived at the northern limit of the great marsh, and, turning eastward, we followed the line of a crooked conduit, in which men were excavating, and from which they sought to irrigate the rice-fields lying just below. We soon came to their water supply in the river Hasbany. This stream is one of the sources of the Jordan, rising in a fine spring some twenty miles to the northward, from which it flows down to this point, where it becomes a mountain torrent, sweeping over its bed of boulders, and "dashing wild and free." Its banks are lined with oleanders, plane trees and agnus-castus, under the foliage of which it hides its current as it speeds on toward the great marsh below. We crossed the Hasbany on a fine old bridge, built of stone, with three massive arches, the structure having an inclined roadway, the highest part being at the western end.

A ride of three miles through a well-wooded country, with an undulating surface, brought us to *Tell el Kâdy*, the ancient site of Dan or Laish. The modern name signifies "the hill of the

[*] Joshua 11 : 1.

judge," and "judge" was the meaning of the word "Dan" among the Israelites. This was the northern limit of the possessions given to the sons of Jacob, as Beersheba was the boundary southward; hence the phrase "from Dan to Beersheba," intended as a description of the whole land.*

The tell, or mound, is of very singular appearance. It is an oblong hill, about twenty-five feet in perpendicular height, and is three hundred yards from north to south, and two hundred and fifty yards from east to west. On its western side a great source of the Jordan sends out a copious stream, almost a full-grown river at once, uniting its waters with those of another stream at the southwest side of the hill. A wonderful fountain, like a large bubbling basin, is here found. Pausing to rest beneath the shadow of an oak or terebinth tree, where the fluttering rags on the branches notified us of the proximity of a sheikh's grave, we sat down for luncheon beside the cool purling stream. It is an enchanting spot, and many events of Old Testament history centre there.

From the earliest times settlers must have been attracted to this place. Sheltered under the side of Mount Hermon, possessing a fountain from

---
* Judges 20 : 1 ; 1 Samuel 3 : 20.

which the drainage of all this part of the mountain seems to find its exit, and having a fertile soil all around, it could not but be attractive to emigrants. Here the people of Laish could dwell at ease, secluded from the world, and separated from their own people at Sidon by the Lebanon mountains. The people of Dan afterward came up this valley on an exploring expedition, and, dispossessing the former occupants, seated themselves in this territory as their own. Their report that this was a "large land," "very good," "a place where there is no want of anything that is in the earth,"* we can still see was correct. And here on this mound, beside the great fountain, they set up their capital, and, as they were far removed from Shiloh, they afterward set up their sanctuary here also. And though Samuel may have forbidden the continuance of this irregular worship in after times, yet it became a so-called "sacred place" when Jeroboam afterward erected a temple here, with the golden calf.† On the southwest corner of the mound, it is said, the golden calf was set up; and as I wandered over this section, I could trace the remains of ancient walls, as of former fortifications or buildings. Just below the hill stood an old mill, now out of repair, and evidently for many years out of use.

* Judges 18 : 9, 10. † 2 Chronicles 13 : 8.

Floods of water rush past its idle wheel, and yet it moves not—an apt illustration of the lack of industry and application on the part of the inhabitants of this favored land. There are many features of interest about Tell el Kâdy, but nothing to excel this great fountain. It is said to be the largest spring in Syria, and is perhaps the largest single fountain in the world. The stream is called by Josephus the Lesser Jordan, is twice as large as the fountain at Banias, and three times as large as the Hasbany, which, though the most distant source of the Jordan, is scarcely anything more than a surface-water stream, while this is a massive volume of water springing out of the earth at one bound.*

* There are two large streams at *Tell el Kâdy*. The largest spring is called '*Ain el Leddân*, and is the one referred to as bursting forth on the west side of the mound, and forming a pool around which are heaped blocks of basaltic rocks. A copious stream runs from this spring and pool. Another stream issues from the southwest side of the mound, perhaps from the same chief source, and soon unites with the former stream, and the two form the *el Leddân*, or as Josephus called it the Little Jordan. The stream from the spring alone contains twice as much water as the stream from the spring at Banias, with which it does not unite in any one stream however, but in several. While the spring at *Tell el Kâdy* is much larger than the spring at Banias, the Banias stream receives water from several other springs, so that the two streams soon after leaving their sources seem to be about equal in volume. As the Banias stream is longer than the *Leddân*, it is usually considered the source of the Jordan. For the *Hasbany* stream is scarcely half the size

As we were reclining under the oak and terebinth, beside the glassy pool, a farmer came that way, carrying his rude plough, made of two saplings, with a wedge-shaped iron point at the foot. He was a worthy successor to the possessions of ancient "Dan." His swarthy complexion, dark eye and prying conduct reminded us of what was said of his ancestor—"Dan shall be a serpent by the way, an adder in the path, that biteth the heels of the horse, so that his rider shall fall backward;" or again, "He shall leap from Bashan," *i. e.*, from the slopes of Hermon, where he is couched watching for his prey.

When Mr. Macgregor was attempting to penetrate the marsh, from a point near Tell el Kâdy, he was set upon by the natives, and pursued from curve to curve around the winding banks of the Jordan, and at last was fired at by one of these worthies, when he surrendered himself, was carried canoe and all to a hut, and kept a prisoner until his escort, hearing of his misfortune, came to his rescue. Our own experience afterward, at Banias, confirmed us in the conviction that the modern inhabitants make good the description of the Danites, as given above.

of the river at its junction with the Jordan. See Conder's *Tent Life*, Prof. Socin, and *Survey of Western Palestine*, vol. i. pp. 96, 105.—*Ed. Am. S. S. Union.*

An hour's ride to the eastward, by a path winding through clumps of oleander and scrub oak, brought us to the town formerly named Panias, now Banias, the Cæsarea Philippi of the New Testament. The men hastened to pitch our camp in a fine grove of olive trees, about one hundred yards distant from the river's bank, and the singular

SOURCES OF THE JORDAN, NEAR BANIAS. (*After Photographs of Frith and Good.*)

interest of the place led us immediately to follow the stream to its source, in the great fountain a short distance above.

Banias stands on a triangular terrace, which rises some five hundred feet above the plain beneath, and abuts on the southwestern spur of Mount Hermon. Just where the terrace joins the spur of the mountain, at its innermost angle, is a cliff of white and pink stone, about eighty feet in height, having carved niches in its ragged front—the marks of an ancient occupation. The fountains stream out of a vast pile of loose stones, about fifty yards distant from the foot of the cliff, and immediately unite in a torrent of limpid water, which goes rushing and roaring past the village, under the ancient arched bridge, down the wady. Were it not for its greater rival at Tell el Kâdy, this fountain would be a marvel indeed. The scenery all around this place is wild and mountainous, and the ancient ruined castle, perched on the height one thousand feet above, adds not a little to the picturesqueness and beauty of the scene. The modern village is situated a short distance from the fountain, and is only a poor mountain hamlet, with dwellings of stone, rudely constructed, not very inviting, nor over cleanly in appearance. Here we saw round huts or booths, built of green branches of trees, and perched upon the house-tops, in which the inhabitants sleep in summer time, in order to escape the fleas with which their houses are infested, or, as others affirm, to escape the serpents and scorpions which abound here.

It was our misfortune to have a difficulty with these troublesome people, who were already handsomely paid for the camping-ground and for the provisions they had furnished us. Our chief dragoman being greatly annoyed by a dog, which persisted in hanging about the tents, picked up a tent mallet, and, poising it, threw it with such precision that he struck the animal in the head, and instantly killed it. Word was carried to the village. The sheikh's son immediately made his appearance, attended by a group of apparent desperadoes, and the protracted quarrel began in due form. All the evening and far into the night the angry dispute continued. We were all warned not to leave the camp, as there might be parties lurking around for personal plunder. Even in going to the river bank just at twilight I was intercepted by a party of men, who menaced me with their fists, and muttered vengeful Arabic at me, which fortunately I could not understand. Careful watch was kept over the camp that night, but no further outbreak occurred until early morning, the hour appointed by our guide for settlement, when the delegation returned. The hour seemed propitious for negotiations, and settlement was made in full for six francs—about one dollar and twenty cents of United States currency.

After the declaration of peace we made another visit to the vicinity of the fountain, and attempted to decipher the mutilated Greek inscription graven in the shell-shaped niche in the face of the cliff, which as some think reads, "The Priest of the

God Pan." If so, this is evidently a relic of the old Greek shrine of Pan, from which the place derives its name, Pan being the Grecian representative of the Syrian god Baal. Quite an extensive cave exists in the cliff near by, which in connection with the fountain made this a suitable spot for the shrine of the sylvan deity.

Of this Josephus writes in connection with his statement that Herod built him a most beautiful temple near the place called Panium, but his description is unlike the present appearance of the place. "This is a very fine cave in a mountain, under which there is a great cavity in the earth, and the cavern is abrupt and prodigiously deep and full of a still water; over it hangs a vast mountain, and under the caverns arise the springs of Jordan. Herod adorned this place, which was already a very remarkable one, still further by the erection of this temple, which was dedicated to Cæsar."

This temple is said to have been erected by Herod the Great in the year 20 B.C., while the one at Samaria, surrounded by the consecrated approach, was completed shortly afterward. He built Herodium, on the Frank Mountain near Bethlehem, from B.C. 20 to 10, Cæsarea on the coast nearly within the same period, and consecrated the temple by which he replaced the humble building of Ezra at Jerusalem, in the year B.C. 14. He was a great builder as well as warrior, and left traces of the magnificence as well as cruelty of his reign in every part of the land.

No remains of the temple are now seen near the fountain, but south of the village we came upon the ruins of three large towers. Climbing to the top of one of these crumbling piles of

BANIAS, OR CÆSAREA-PHILIPPI. (*After Photographs of Frith and Good.*)

masonry, we noticed the remains of a large arched bridge adjacent; but it did not seem to be as ancient as the one spanning the fountain torrent near our camping-ground. "Here," it has been said, "are the ruins of the once-famed frontier city Cæsarea-Philippi. Here were the villas of the Roman settlers, and in their midst stood the public theatre, where Titus on his return from the capture of Jerusalem held a great festival, and compelled the captive Jews to act as gladiators and fight with wild beasts in the public arena."

Josephus, who is our authority for many particulars in the lives of the Herods, affirms that Philip, who afterward succeeded to the town and districts around, proved that Lake Phiala, situated some four hours distant to the southeast upon the mountain heights, was the source whence this fountain is supplied in an occult manner. Philip "had chaff thrown into Phiala, and it was found at Panium, where the ancients thought the fountain-head of the river was, whither it had been therefore carried."* It is hardly necessary to add that it has been proved by modern scientists that no connection exists between Phiala and the fountain at Banias, and at present there is not a drop of water in the cavern at the latter place, the stream now issuing from a pile of loose stones at quite a distance from the cliff, as already stated. Notwithstanding the alleged experiment of Philip, Banias is now regarded as the most eastern source of the Jordan; and though the former architectural grandeur of the place is now fallen into hopeless ruin and decay, yet the natural beauty remains. Dean Stanley calls it the Syrian Tivoli, and Canon Tristram, with his usual regard to natural beauty, writes: "Everywhere

---

* *Wars:* Book III. 10 : 7.

there is a wild medley of cascades, mulberry trees, fig trees, dashing torrents, festoons of vines, bubbling fountains, reeds and ruins, and the mingled music of birds and waters."

But above all it must be remembered that Jesus came into the town of Cæsarea-Philippi with his disciples before he took with him Peter and James and John into the high mountain apart and was transfigured before them. This, at least, was the northernmost limit of our Lord's travels. It was not unsuitable that here, upon the spur which runs like a graded way to the snow-clad heights of majestic Hermon, the glory of the Master should be revealed to the wondering disciples. Here, at the source of that sacred stream which is inseparably associated with the history and poetry of the two dispensations, it was fitting that the divinity of our Lord should be first openly announced, from whence it might spread through all lands in coming time, " Thou art the Christ, the Son of the living God."

Our travel in the Holy Land was now completed. True we were yet to see Damascus, Baalbec, the Lebanon mountains and Beyrout, whence we were to sail for Asia Minor, Constantinople and Greece. It was to be our privilege also to visit many of the sites of cities famous in classic annals, and consecrated by the labors of the apostles and fathers in the Christian Church. But the land of the patriarchs, judges, kings and prophets we were now to leave behind us. And as we passed up the heights of Hermon we cast a parting glance over the wide valley of the Jordan, and took our final leave of the "Promised Land," which Moses longed to enter, but only saw from a distance; since hallowed by the Saviour's feet, now "trodden under foot of the Gentiles," awaiting the dawn of a brighter and better day.

INDEX.

	PAGE
Abraham with Isaac,	202
Absalom's tomb,	132, 135
African fish in Galilee,	321
Ai, Location of,	197
'Ain Bârideh,	296
'Ain Belata,	329
'Ain Duk,	190
'Ain el Mellaha,	326
'Ain es Sultan,	181, 192
'Ain et Tin, Fountain of,	316
'Ain Feshkha,	187
Ajalon, Valley of,	41
American legation,	121
Anathoth, Distant view of,	154
Anderson, Lieut., at Nablus,	217
Andromeda, Story of,	15
Antiquities at Banias,	345
Capernaum,	310
Samaria,	229
Tiberias,	289
Antonia, Tower of,	71
Apples of Sodom,	181
Aqueduct at Tabighah,	307
Baca, Valley of,	200, 203
Banias, Ruins at,	341, 345
Baptism in the Jordan,	175
Bathing in the Dead Sea,	171
Jordan River,	172
Beersheba,	102, 337
Bees making honey,	107
Beit el Khulil,	96, 106
Ben Hur, source of legend,	276
Bethany,	136
Bethel,	196
Bethesda, note,	69
Beth-horon, View of,	41
Bethlehem,	108
Church of Nativity,	109
inn and manger,	50
view eastward,	113
Bethphage,	136
Bethsaida in Galilee,	307
Julias,	287
Birds of Palestine,	184, 266, 319

	PAGE
Boat in Galilee,	294, 309
Booth on house-top,	342
Bread like a stone,	271
Buffalo in the Huleh,	328
Calvary,	127
Camp at Gennesaret,	319
at Jericho,	183
life,	332
Canal from Haifa to Zerin,	321
Capernaum, Tell Hum,	311
Fountain of,	316
Carmel, Mount,	246, 260
Carpenter at Nazareth,	264
Cascades at Banias,	347
Cave at Banias,	344
of the Nativity, Bethlehem,	110
Cæsarea, on the coast,	344
Philippi,	341
Chamber, Upper, of the Last Supper,	120
Chinnereth, Lake of,	286
Chorazin,	262, 312
Christ, Ascension of,	139
asleep upon pillow,	295
at Sea of Galilee,	317
at the garden and Calvary,	127, 135
at the well in Samaria,	210
birth at Bethlehem,	110
weeping over Jerusalem,	136, 163
youth at Nazareth,	264
Church of the Holy Sepulchre,	122
Coffee served by a smithy,	197
Colonization of Palestine,	19
Colonnade at Samaria,	228
Corner stone of temple wall,	66
Crusaders at Ramleh,	39
Dalmanutha,	297
Dan,	336
Dancing at Jerusalem and Shiloh,	161, 209

David's street,	121
tomb, traditional,	120
Dead Sea,	168, 186
Deborah's victory,	244
Deir Diwan,	195
Dining under difficulties,	49
Dorcas, Tomb of,	24
Dothan,	233
Dress of men and women,	263
Earthquake at Tiberias,	282
Ebal,	212
El Aksa, Mosque of,	66
El Karey, Visit from,	214
El Kubab,	40
El Lisan,	188
Elijah at Wady Kelt,	190
Emmaus, Kûlonieh,	51
En Rogel, Well of,	66, 130
Encounter with Arabs,	343
Endor,	245
Eriha, Village of,	177, 191
Erinna, the monk of Mount Tabor,	275
Esdraelon, Plain of,	240, 260
Eshcol, Vineyards of,	104
Etam, Site of,	107
Farmers at Dan,	340
Miseries of,	242
Farm-houses secluded,	28, 94
Fevers at Tabighah,	315
Fish abundant in Galilee,	308, 320
Fishermen at Tiberias,	291, 309
Fishermen's tents and traps,	309
Flowers at Nazareth,	266
among Judean hills,	91
Food of the people,	329
Fountain at Banias,	342
at Dan,	239
at Nazareth,	257
at Shiloh,	209
of Elisha,	181, 192
of the Virgin, at Jerusalem,	70
Sealed,	86
Frank Mountain,	114
Gate of the glen,	41
Gazelle,	194
Gennesaret, Plain of,	298
Gerizim, View from,	213
German colony,	20
Gethsemane, Garden of,	58, 135

Ghâwarineh, Tribe of,	177
Gibeah of Saul,	153
Gibeon,	147
Gideon's army,	245
Gilboa, Mountains of,	244, 260
Gilead,	186
Gilgal, Eriha,	177
Girl surprised at the khan,	49
Girls, Hard lot of,	225
Golden Gate, Jerusalem,	69
Grain field trampled on,	92
Grasshoppers,	280
Haifa, Port of,	259
Hand-mills,	335
Hanina, Valley of,	51
Haram esh Sherif,	61
Hasbany River,	336
Hazor, Site of,	336
Hebron, City of,	96
Hospice of,	101
Mosque of,	98
Hermits at Mt. Quarantania,	189
Hermon, Mount,	347
Herod Antipas,	287
the Great, buildings, etc.,	344
Herodium at Frank Mountain,	114
Hezekiah, Pool of,	121
Hill-top at Nazareth,	259
Hinnom, Valley of,	79, 130
Hoffman, Rev. C., Colony of,	20
Holy Sepulchre at Jerusalem,	122
Ceremonies at,	127
Horses at Jaffa,	20, 22
Houses at Nazareth,	262
Huleh, Lake of,	228, 334
Hulbul,	94
Hymns about Jordan,	177
Inscriptions at Banias,	343
Irrigation from the Hasbany,	336
Jabbok,	194
Jackals,	182, 201
Jacob's ladder,	198
well, note,	210-218
Jaffa described,	13, 17, 18
Jehoshaphat, Valley of,	131
Jenin, Village of,	234
Jeremiah's grotto,	158
Jericho, Site of,	185, 190
Jeroboam's calf worship,	338
Jerome's grotto at Bethlehem,	111
Jerusalem, Arrival at,	53

INDEX. 351

	PAGE
Jerusalem, Population of,	54
Streets of,	57
Jesus at Nazareth,	268
never at Tiberias,	289
Jezebel and Ahab,	247
Jezreel,	242
Jordan described,	172, 176
Length of,	293
plain,	194
Source of,	337
Joseph's tomb,	211
Josephus describes Banias,	344
Gennesaret,	299
Jericho,	190
Samaria,	230
Tiberias,	288
Joshua at Ai,	192, 197
reading the law at Shechem,	212
Judea, Hill country of,	52, 85
Judges, Tomb of the,	144
Judith and Holofernes,	232
Kades in Galilee,	329
Keble's lines on Jordan,	293
Kelt, Brook of, Cherith,	166, 178, 190
Kerak, outlet of Galilee,	292
Khan described,	48
Minieh,	302
of Good Samaritan,	164
Yûsef,	322
Khurbet en Nasara,	105
Kirjath-jearim,	45, 47
Kishon River,	240
Kûlonieh described,	51
Kustul,	50
Lake of Galilee,	304
Last view of,	322
Names of,	286
Sacred associations of,	317
View of,	285
Lapping water,	226
Law, Place of reading,	212
Lazarus, Tomb of,	137
Lepers and dwellings,	130, 143
Lord's Supper, Place of,	120
Lydda viewed from Ramleh,	34
Maccabees, Home of,	42
Macgregor attacked,	340
Magdala,	297
Maimonides, Tomb of,	293
Mar Elias, Monastery,	80

	PAGE
Mary's kitchen at Nazareth,	256
Merom, Waters of,	327
Mill in operation,	327
Miracle of loaves and fishes,	296
Mishna composed at Tiberias,	283
Moab, Hills of,	194
Mohammedan superstitions,	167
Montefiore's garden,	20
Moriah, Sights on,	64
Mosque el Aksa,	66
Mound at Dan,	337
Mount of Beatitudes,	277
Mudauwarah, Fountain of,	300
Nablûs, Village of,	214, 221, 226
Nain, Village of,	250
Nativity, Church of, Bethlehem,	109
Nazareth,	255, 268
Reflections on leaving,	267
Neby Samwil,	145
Needle's eye in gate,	160
Nob,	154
Oak at Dan,	337
Oak of Abraham,	101
Oleanders,	296, 301
Olives, Mount of,	61, 134, 139
Omar, Mosque of,	63, 65
Orange orchards at Jaffa,	24
Pan, the Syrian Baal,	344
Papyrus,	328, 334
Partridges,	201
Passover attended,	140
Peter's vision at Jaffa,	16
Phiala, Lake of,	346
Philistia, Coast of,	9
Ploughing of Elisha,	325
Ploughs and ploughing,	93
Precipitation, Mount of,	252, 257
Procession in David's Street,	161
Quarantania, Mount of Temptation,	177, 189
Rabbis at Tiberias,	283, 293
Rachel's Tomb, note,	81
Ramet el Khulil,	96
Ramleh, History of,	39
Tower of,	33
Reed flute,	327
shaken by the wind,	175
Rephaim, Plain of,	79

352   INDEX.

	PAGE		PAGE
Road, Old Roman,	193	Sycamore tree at Jericho,	190
Roads lacking in Palestine,	80		
Rob Roy on the Jordan,	340	Tabighah, Bethsaida, 305,	316
Robbers' caverns,	298	Tabor, Mount, 250,	271
Rock, Sacred, on Mount Mo-		Tell Hum, Capernaum,	310
riah,	64	Temple at Banias,	344
Roses of Sharon,	28	at Jerusalem,	72
Round fountain at Gennesaret,	300	Terebinth tree, 207,	209
Ruin at Shiloh,	206	Thief, penitent, Home of,	42
		Threshing-floor,	92
Safed, city on hill, 279,	322	Tiberias, City of, 280,	294
Samaria, Hill of, 227,	231	Titus at Banias,	345
Samaritan, The Good,	164	at Kerak,	292
Samaritans' synagogue, 213,	222	Tomb of David,	120
Sânûr, Bethulia,	232	of Moses,	166
Scopus, 144,	154	of the Judges,	144
Sharon, Plain of,	28	of the Kings,	154
Rose of,	34	Tower of David, Jerusalem,	119
Shechem, Ancient,	223	Towers of Banias,	345
Sheikhs as guides,	164	Traditions of Mohammedans,	323
Shepherds and sheep,	90	Transfiguration, Place of, 273,	347
Shepherds' fields, Bethlehem,	113		
Shiloh, 204,	209	Via Dolorosa,	74
Shunem,	248	Vineyards at Hebron, 102,	104
Siloam,	131	Volcanic traces at Galilee, 290,	321
Village of,	130		
Simon the tanner's house,	14	Wailing place of the Jews,	74
Singing of girls at 'Ain Duk,	192	War over a dog,	342
Sinjil,	203	Warm springs, Tiberias,	290
Sirocco, in plain of Huleh,	330	Weeding wheat, 210,	248
Sodom and Gomorrah,	188	Weeping over Jerusalem, 136,	163
Solomon's pools, 86,	107	Well of David, Bethlehem,	114
porch,	68	Wilderness of Judea,	186
stables,	66	Women grinding at mill,	335
quarries,	158	of Sychar,	210
Songs of native girls,	191	Poverty of, 210, 214,	225
Sower, Parable of,	315	wailing at the grave,	83
Stone at the Sepulchre,	156		
Stones, Foundation of temple,	67	Zacharias, Tomb of,	132
St. Stephen's gate, View from,	58	Zion, Hill of,	119

www.ingramcontent.com/pod-product-compliance
Lightning Source LLC
Chambersburg PA
CBHW030305240426
43673CB00040B/1061